Travel, Sabbatical, and Study Leave Policies in College Libraries
CLIP Note #30

Compiled by

Carolyn Gaskell
Walla Walla College
College Place, Washington

Allen S. Morrill
Massachusetts College of Liberal Arts
North Adams, Massachusetts

College Library Information Packet Committee
College Libraries Section
Association of College and Research Libraries
A Division of the American Library Association
Chicago 2001

The paper used in this publication meets the minimum requirements of American National Standard for Information Sciences–Permanence of Paper for Printed Library Materials, ANSI Z39.48-1992. ∞

Library of Congress Cataloging-in-Publication Data
Gaskell, Carolyn.
   Travel, sabbatical, and study leave policies in college libraries / compiled by Carolyn Gaskell, Allen S. Morrill.
       p. cm. -- (CLIP note ; #30
Includes bibliographical references.
   ISBN 0-8389-8164-X (alk. paper)
1. Academic libraries--Employees--Salaries, etc.--United States. 2. College librarians--Salaries, etc.--United States. 3. Travel costs--United States. 4. Leave of absence--United States. 5. Library surveys--United States. I. Morrill, Allen S. II. CLIP notes ; #30.
   Z675.U5 G386 2001
   027.7'0973--dc21
                                  2001041325

Printed on recycled paper.

Printed in the United States of America.

05 04 03 02 01   5 4 3 2 1

CONTENTS

CLIP Notes Committee

Lewis R. Miller, Chair
Irwin Library
Butler University
Indianapolis, IN

Janice Bandelin
James B. Duke Library
Furman University
Greenville, South Carolina

Roxann R. Bustos
Reese Library
Augusta State University
Augusta, Georgia

Jody L. Caldwell
Drew University Libraries
Drew University
Madison, New Jersey

Doralyn H. Edwards
University of Wyoming Libraries
University of Wyoming
Laramie, Wyoming

Jamie Hastreiter
William Luther Cobb Library
Eckerd College
St. Petersburg, FL

David A. Wright
Speed Library
Mississippi College
Clinton, Mississippi

The compilers wish to recognize the efforts of Jamie Hastreiter in bringing this volume to publication. Her persistence and editorial skills were invaluable in the development and completion of this project.

INTRODUCTION

Objective

The *College Library Information Packet (CLIP) Note* series is well known for providing "college and small university libraries with state-of-the-art reviews and current documentation on library practices and procedures of relevance to them."[1] The College Libraries Section of the Association of College and Research Libraries sponsors the series. This *CLIP Note* provides information and sample policies on travel, sabbaticals, and study leaves of absence in small academic libraries.

Background

As librarians seek to expand their knowledge and keep up with current trends, attending conferences and workshops and taking sabbaticals and study leaves becomes increasingly more important. In addition, the number and array of conferences and workshops librarians and library staff have to choose from has increased appreciably. Some librarians must not only attend but also participate in such educational events for a favorable annual review or to be eligible for tenure, promotion, or advancement in rank. This *CLIP Note* was designed to examine and present practices and policies in college libraries regarding travel, sabbaticals, and study leaves.

Librarians are expected to keep up-to-date with library policies and practices and to keep current with new trends and technological changes. Through the years, ACRL guidelines for college libraries have consistently included statements of expectation that both librarians and staff should have opportunities for continuing education and participation in professional organizations.[2] Librarians with rank and tenure are expected to publish articles and/or books and to contribute to their professional associations and organizations in a manner similar to their colleagues in other disciplines. To engage in these activities, librarians need sabbatical and study leave time as well as travel support. The traditional areas of librarianship have split into numerous specialties while computer and other technologies have expanded the responsibilities and knowledge requirements of librarians and their staffs. In this climate, librarians attempting to keep current in their fields find an increasing array of conferences to attend. Library administrators use many avenues to stretch scarce resources and/or reduce costs for obtaining materials, automation services, databases, and other resources. For example, libraries are participating in various user councils, groups and/or multiple consortia. As they do so, they find that the expectation for participation in the administration of those entities has increased for both

---

[1] P. Grady Morein, "What is a CLIP Note?" *College and Research Libraries News* 46 (May 1985): 226.

[2] "ACRL Standards for College Libraries 2000 Edition: Staff," ACRL College Libraries Section Standards Committee, 2000 [http://www.ala.org/acrl/guides/college.html#staff].

librarians and library staff. Consequently, there is an increased need for travel funds to meet these increased expectations. Similarly, the need for sabbatical and time for study leaves has also increased.

Costs associated with attending a conference have also risen sharply in the last few years. A study of American Library Association registration fees and hotel rates as reported in *American Libraries* from 1992 to 2000 illustrates this point (Table 1). During those years, conference on-site registration fees increased from $98 to $195 (99%). Pre-registration fees increased from $85 to $125 (47%). In the area of lodging, the most expensive hotel rooms have stayed about the same, with only a $29 difference from 1992 to 2000. This represents a 19% increase in the luxury rooms. Over the same period, however, the least expensive rooms increased

Date	City	Cost	Advance Cost	Hotel Highest	Hotel Lowest	Average Single	Average Most/least Expensive
1992	San Francisco	98	85	150	65	113.76	107.50
1993	New Orleans	98	85	174	88	107.24	131.00
1994	Miami	103	90	155	60	104.12	107.50
1995	Chicago	103	90	165	85	130.55	125.00
1996	New York	140	105	205	99	159.83	152.00
1997	San Francisco	175	105	169	85	134.30	127.00
1998	Washington	185	135	169	80	128.89	124.50
1999	New Orleans	195	125	175	69	174.15	122.00
2000	Chicago	195	125	179	85	146.83	132.00
	$ Change	$97	$40	$29	$20	$33	$24
	% Change	99%	47%	19%	31%	29%	23%

Table 1
Average Costs by City & Hotels

in price from $65 to $85, which was an increase 31%! In addition, the number of conference hotel rooms under $99 has diminished significantly. In 1992, at the San Francisco conference, there were over 700 rooms available for under $99. At the 2000 Chicago conference, there were only 100 rooms available at this rate. It is unrealistic to expect conference fees to remain static, or for hotel rates to stay the same. Increases in these items are natural. However, such costs have increased significantly over this eight-year period. For the attendee whose supporting library is unable to fund such increases, conference attendance could become particularly difficult.

Not unexpectedly, interest in this topic is increasing. For example, in the period from February 2000 to February 2001, at least four separate queries posted to the COLLIB-L ListServ included questions about funding for conference and workshop attendance, methods of funding allocation for such attendance, release time, and tuition benefits for continuing education classes. The two earliest requests were in February and March of 2000. They focused on tuition and benefits such as professional development days. Out of 140 responses to the latter survey, 110 libraries indicated there was no limit on the time librarians could take to attend workshops and conferences. This survey also found that out of 141 responses, 114 libraries did not have unions of any type, a conclusion with which results from this *CLIP Note* survey concur.[3]

---

[3]Priya Rai, "Summary of Benefits Survey," Online posting. 16 March 2000. COLLIB-L@acs.wooster.edu.

The two most recent requests for information occurred in November 2000 and February 2001. Nineteen libraries responded to the 2001 request. The most interesting data from this brief survey is to be found under question eight which asked participants to list the advantages and disadvantages of their current system for distributing travel money. Under "disadvantages," comments such as the following were given: "more librarians than money"; "costs keep increasing, but budget does not"; and "more people wishing to travel and the increase of need for skills development." When asked for recommendations, these were some of the suggestions provided: "More money"; "increased funding, better system for demonstrating effectiveness of expenditures"; "insist the dean ask for and receive more funds"; "more money for a higher percentage of funding"; "would like to have a base budget rather than using salary savings"; and "more money."[4]

Library funds to support increased travel seem to have, at the very least, remained static. Such limited funds require an equitable means of fund allocation. Written policies provide librarians and library administrators with consistent, equitable methods of allocating travel funds and/or granting sabbatical and study leaves, especially in a time of static or diminished funding. Rationale for granting sabbaticals and study leaves can also be included within these documents. College library administrators could also benefit from the development of such policies. Therefore, this *CLIP Note*, which covers travel policies, sabbaticals, and study leaves of absence, is designed to assist library administrators facing these questions and enable them to design new or better travel polices of their own. The data and sample policies should provide information with which library administrations can sway academic administrators to specifically include librarians in sabbatical and study leave policies.

Literature Survey

A 1978 survey of thirty-five ACRL libraries was the earliest mentioned study on the topic of travel policies discovered in the literature survey.[5] Another study was published in 1980 as *Travel Policies of Twenty-One College and University Libraries*."[6] Since then, three articles or compilations on travel policies, mostly in ARL libraries, have appeared. No study seems to have focused primarily on college and small university libraries.

The three most pertinent articles or compilations are the 1980 *Travel Policies of Twenty-One College and University Libraries*,[7] the 1989 *Survey of Travel Support Policies at ARL*

---

[4]Jen Phillips, "Travel Policies – replies," Online posting. 12 February 2001. COLLIB-L@acs.wooster.edu.

[5]Winberta Yao. "Travel Funds Committees," *College and Research Libraries News* 41(December 1980): 330.

[6]Chicago: Association of College and Research Libraries, 1980.

[7]Ibid.

Libraries,[8] and the 1990 *Travel Policies in ARL Libraries.*[9] It has been over ten years since the last article or compilation specifically on travel policies in libraries appeared.

Institutions canvassed during the earliest published (1980) survey included four colleges, two college systems, and three community colleges, the rest were universities. "One-third (34 of 100) of the libraries questioned reported having written policy statements that specify criteria for awarding travel funds and reimbursements."[10] Those libraries lacking written policies indicated that they planned to develop them in the future. The publication consists of a short abstract, a reproduction of the 1980 *C&RL News* item cited earlier, and the twenty-one policies.

Blomberg and Chapman's 1989 survey was more extensive and provided significant analysis. Of 118 surveys sent to ARL library directors in the United States and Canada, 90 were returned, for a 76.3% response rate. The authors received thirty-three travel polices for study and comparison. They found that many libraries made a distinction between administrative and professional development travel. Release time was generously given in most cases, but often, librarians were required to produce some type of report upon their return from travel. At most libraries, a committee handled travel requests. In conclusion, the authors provide a profile of an "average" ARL library's travel policy.[11]

Cramer's survey, conducted in 1989, canvassed 103 ARL libraries. He received 73 responses for a 71% return rate. Thirteen policies, all from major and mostly state universities, were provided as examples. It was an update of the "small section on travel support addressed in SPEC Kit #86, *Professional Development in ARL Libraries*, published in 1982."[12] Instead of distinguishing between administrative and professional development travel, this study distinguished between travel "required to promote or improve job-related skills ('professional development') and travel undertaken to attend conferences ('career involvement')."[13] The greatest similarities were found in the origin of travel funds–the library's budget. In some cases, though, institutional funds were also available. The area in which most libraries differed was the manner in which the allocation process occurred. Cramer also noted that there had been an increase in the number of professional conferences and pre-and post workshops held for continuing education in the 1980's.[14]

---

[8]Donna Pittman Blomberg and Karen Chapman, "Survey of Travel Support Policies at ARL Libraries," *The Journal of Academic Librarianship* 15 (May 1989): 90-93.

[9]Michael D. Cramer, *Travel Policies in ARL Libraries.* SPEC Kit 161 (Washington D.C.: Association of Research Libraries: Office of Management Studies; ED 330 353, 1990), microfiche.

[10]*Travel Policies of Twenty-One College and University Libraries* (Chicago: Association of College and Research Libraries, 1980), i.

[11]Blomberg and Chapman, "Survey of Travel Support Policies," 91-92.

[12]Cramer, *Travel Policies*, fiche 4.

[13]Ibid., fiche 1.

[14]Ibid.

Questions asked on the various travel surveys described above were quite similar and fall into the following categories:

Source of funds
Authority to allocate funds
Activities covered by funds
Limits on funding
Staff covered

Other literature surveyed discussed the reasons for travel, sabbaticals, and study leaves. The earliest article we were able to find that mentions sabbaticals and leaves was published in 1970. It focused on benefits for librarians and library staff. At that time, sabbaticals and leaves of absence were associated with vacation time, sick leave, and funeral leave. Responses to the author's queries indicated that sabbaticals and leaves of absence were among the lowest benefits on their list of priorities. Brief mention was made of attendance at professional conferences, but little substantive data was provided. The author did recommend that professional travel policies should be developed.[15]

Almost twenty years later, Wilding in his article "Career and Staff Development: A Convergence," makes the case for library administrators to encourage the growth and career advancement of their librarians and staff. Like Cramer, Wilding also makes the distinction between professional growth and career advancement. While he agrees that the former is keeping up-to-date with current trends and issues, he defines the latter as obtaining additional credentials that allow upward mobility. Not surprisingly, Wilding includes funding support as one of the responsibilities of the library administration. He further makes the point that fund allocation should not be weighted towards those who are on committees or giving papers since that most often excludes younger members who are in greater need of the learning experiences offered at conferences, workshops, and other professional meetings.[16]

Data on sabbaticals and study leaves, as reported in *Criteria for Promotion and Tenure for Academic Librarians,* revealed that of 155 respondents, librarians at 92 institutions (59%) were eligible for sabbaticals. Of those sabbaticals, 79 or 51% were the same length as faculty, 67 or 43% were not the same length, and 9 or 6% were indicated as other options. Also, of 121 respondents, 88 or 73% were required to demonstrate scholarship for promotion or tenure.[17] In most cases, librarians worked under the same definition of scholarship as did the faculty.

---

[15]James Wright, "Fringe Benefits for Academic Library Personnel," *College and Research Libraries* 31 (January 1970): 18-21.

[16]Thomas L. Wilding, "Career and staff development: A convergence," *C & RL News* 50 (November 1989): 899-902.

[17]Virginia Vesper and Gloria Kelley, *Criteria for Promotion and Tenure for Academic Librarians: CLIP Note #26* (Chicago: College Libraries Section, Association of College and Research Libraries, a division of the American Library Association, 1997): 23-25.

Leadership in library associations, presentations at conferences, and attendance at conferences and workshops, were all mentioned as being expected for advancement.[18]

Leaves of absence are most often mentioned in the literature as parts of personnel manuals, faculty handbooks, or in collective bargaining agreements (65 agreements were retrieved in a February 2001 ERIC search). Other articles, such as that by Daniel F. Ring, describe leave programs at individual institutions. He equates study leaves with the arrival of full faculty status for academic librarians and indicates that it is scholarly activity that aligns librarians most with faculty.[19] Other articles, such as that by Kee DeBoer and Wendy Culotta surveyed libraries on faculty status. Their study drew on literature published during the1980's. One of their questions pertained to sabbaticals. They found that librarians most likely to be eligible for sabbaticals were from the Rocky Mountain region (85%) and those least likely from Ohio (49%). Their query on research activities indicated that release time was available 67% of the time for professional activities, but only 20% for research.[20] Several earlier studies on faculty status, also including sabbatical leaves, were cited.

Survey Procedures

Standard *CLIP Note* procedures were followed for this project. In January of 2000 a preliminary survey was designed and used to canvass selected libraries on the west and east coasts. In checking for documents, there were only 3.5 respondents per every 10 who had some sort of travel policy, a low 35% return rate. Consequently, it was deemed best to enlarge the scope of the study to include sabbaticals and study leaves of absence. Subsequently, the survey was devised to obtain information not only on travel, but also on sabbatical and study leave policies. Many of the questions were based on those asked in the1989 Blomberg study. In addition, two questions on sabbaticals and leaves were included from the *CLIP Note* study on promotion and tenure.[21]

The questionnaire was designed to collect standard information describing the libraries in the sample (size, enrollment, etc.). Also included was a section on how rank and tenure are handled. It seems logical that those institutions where librarians hold academic or faculty rank would also require a higher degree of involvement in the profession through participation in library associations, committee work and attendance at professional conferences. Since staff members play an important role in the optimum operation of libraries, staff requirements for keeping current in their fields is also addressed.

---

[18]Vesper and Kelly, *Criteria for Promotion and Tenure*, 8.

[19]Daniel F. Ring, "Professional Development Leave As A Stepping Stone to Faculty Status," *The Journal of Academic Librarianship* 4 (March 1978): 19-20.

[20]Kee DeBoer and Wendy Culotta, "The Academic Librarian and Faculty Status in the 1980s: A Survey of the Literature," *College and Research Libraries* 48 (May 1987): 218.

[21] Vesper and Kelly, *Criteria for Promotion and Tenure*, 23-24.

The *CLIP Note* committee reviewed the draft survey and made suggestions. The final, approved survey was distributed in May 2000 to the 267 libraries that were then members of the *CLIP Note* survey pool. In August, a reminder card followed the initial survey posting to those institutions that had not yet returned the survey. In all, 125 surveys were returned for a 47% return rate. The survey was sent out a bit later than usual. Normally, *CLIP Note* surveys are sent out earlier in the school year. Conflict with summer vacations may be a major reason that the return rate was lower than expected.

Sample policies have been drawn from those provided by the respondents. Selected policies meet the following criteria:

Concise and clearly written
Universal interest (as opposed to policies addressing specific issues which may not be
    applicable to other institutions)
Permission to publish the policy in this *CLIP Note*

ANALYSIS OF SURVEY RESULTS

General Institutional Information
(Questions 1-12)

The current survey was sent to 267 institutions of which 125 responded for a 47% response rate. It elicited fifty-one policies, twenty-six of which are reproduced in this *CLIP Note*. To date, the current study has surveyed the largest number of libraries on the issue of travel policies and is the only one focused on college and small university libraries. Responses from private colleges outnumbered those from public institutions almost four to one (99 vs. 26). The typical college and small university library employs seven librarians, five equivalent professionals, and fifteen support staff. These are the individuals affected by the data included in this report.

Eighty-three percent of the libraries responding have library level travel budgets averaging $6,018. The smallest budgets ranged from $80 to $550. Twelve libraries have library travel budgets less than $1,000. In contrast, the largest library travel budget was $21,684. Four libraries reported travel budgets in excess of $20,000. Comparatively, Blomberg and Chapman's study found that 80% of the ARL libraries had a library level professional travel budget[22] and Cramer's 70%.[23] Results of this survey indicate that far fewer college and small university libraries, only 21%, have separate administrative travel budgets.

---

[22]Blomberg and Chapman, "Survey of Travel Support Policies," 91.
[23]Cramer, *Travel Policies*, fiche 4.

We compared the number of libraries providing travel funding to the number which require keeping current in the field. The data indicated that librarians (83%), other professionals (72%), and support staff (57%) were all required to remain current in their fields. Travel support for maintaining this currency was provided at a majority (85%) of the institutions.

Rank, Tenure, and Continuing Education (Questions 13-15)

Less than half of the librarians in the sample (45%) have faculty status and even fewer (30%) have academic rank, which brings with it some faculty privileges. However, a combination of those figures found that 75% of librarians hold some type of faculty privileges while a similar percentage, 79%, are required to remain current in their fields. In view of the number of librarians holding faculty rank or academic status, it would have been expected that continuing education experiences should have a fairly substantial impact on promotion in rank and/or tenure. Indeed, the data show that 83% of the librarians are required to remain current in their fields, 72% must engage in continuing education for promotion and 80% must do so for their annual performance review.

The area in which continuing education has the least affect is tenure. Only 47% indicated that continuing education was a requirement in this area. The survey did not specifically ask how many librarians actually held tenure, so there is no data to indicate whether the low number for tenure is due to few academic librarians holding tenure or some other factor. Similarly, Blomberg found that "In more than 90 percent of ARL libraries surveyed, participation in professional organizations is a factor in job evaluations."[24] She also found that having tenure did not seem to make a difference.

In regards to other professional staff, the numbers are much lower. Only 4% hold either faculty status or academic rank. Instead, about half (52%) hold either administrative or staff status. Yet, almost three-quarters are expected to remain current in their fields (72%) and demonstrate continuing education experiences for their annual performance reviews (73%). If we look ahead and compare this data with the findings from question twenty-three, the data indicate that these other professionals have the least travel support, less even than support staff.

Ten institutions answered question fifteen. Of those, only nine indicated that promotion was governed by a union contract. Four institutions responded that other professionals were governed by a union contract and six indicated that staff was so governed. Questions thirty-seven and thirty-eight also indicate a low level of union contracts covering sabbatical leaves. Such results indicate that, among those college and small university libraries responding to this survey, there are few union shops to affect the privileges and responsibilities of any level of library staff.

---

[24]Blomberg and Chapman, "Survey of Travel Support Policies," 92.

Travel Policies, Compensatory Time, and Administrative Travel (Questions 16-22)

Travel Policies

Few of the responding libraries (44%), have institutional travel policies that cover librarians. In comparsion, the 1980 study found that only one-third of the ARL libraries had written travel policies. So, slightly more small college libraries are now covered by institutional travel policies than were ARL libraries in 1980. However, there are few written library level policies. Therefore, as might be expected, question eighteen indicated that the majority of policies, 80% (96 of 120) are unwritten. It would seem logical then, that the response to question twenty-four which asked who determines the distribution of funds, was overwhelmingly the library director (82%). This continues the pattern established in question nine in which the majority of libraries indicated that they have a line item for travel in their operating budgets. Travel funds located within the library's budget should give library administrators more local control of who attends conferences and other meetings. Unwritten policies also govern staff travel in 75% of the institutions reporting. Few institutional or library level policies govern travel for other library professionals.

Since written policies afford a standardized and fair method of administering the library's travel budget, why do so many library administrators rely on unwritten policies? Comments that were submitted for question twenty-one provide a clue. Of the twenty-one comments received, here are a representative few:

"Some things are better left unwritten. It's more flexible that way."
"Don't feel we are large enough to need it. Travel needs are being met without a policy."
"We're small and trust each other to do the right thing."
"We have the flexibility of meeting the needs of the library this way."
"Travel budget is too unpredictable from year-to-year."

Perhaps the answer lies in unpredictable budgets and the need for flexibility in choosing which of the changing array of meetings to attend each year. Another factor could be the small number of librarians (seven on average) who staff these institutions.

Compensatory Time

Blomberg found that compensatory or release time was provided liberally at the ARL libraries.[25] Does this hold true for college and small university libraries? Data indicate that 120

---

[25] Blomberg and Chapman, "Survey of Travel Support Policies," 92.

or 97% of libraries do provide compensatory or release time to librarians. Other library professionals (76 or 93%) and support staff (115 or 95%) also receive this benefit.

Administrative Travel Budget

As indicated in the section on general institutional information, data on administrative travel collected by this survey indicates a major departure from prior studies of ARL libraries. Those studies found that administrative and professional development travel funds were separated in most libraries. However, out of the 124 libraries from colleges and small universities which responded to this question on the recent survey, 98 or 79% indicated that their libraries did not have a separate administrative budget and neither did their institutions (103 or 83% of 121 responses). This is an important difference since administrative travel is often fully funded. Of the 44 libraries who do have separate funds, the average amount available for administrative travel is $2,740. If professional development travel is competing with administrative travel, that competition could mean fewer funds are available for professional development.

Activities Covered by Travel Policies
(Questions 23-24; 32)

What Elements of Travel are Funded?

This question did not differentiate between written and unwritten travel policies. Answers are based on library level policies for 46% of the institutions reporting. Institutional policies were used 29% of the time and in 23% of the cases, responses are based on both an institutional and a library level policy.

Registration fees, airfare, lodging, and mileage for use of one's own car were expenses most likely to be covered for librarians, other professionals, and support staff alike. Meals, or per diem, was the next expense most likely to be reimbursed. This data compares favorably to that reported by Blomberg and Cramer.[26] Comparing the level of support received by various library staff, however, the data indicate that Librarians received the most support for all types of travel.

Purposes for Travel

Librarians at 30% of the reporting libraries are able to choose between a variety of national, regional, and local conventions, meetings, conferences, etc. For the rest, funding for national or regional library conventions is most likely to be approved (85% and 84%

---

[26] Blomberg and Chapman, "Survey of Travel Support Policies," 92 and Cramer, *Travel Policies*, fiche 9.

respectively). For other library professionals and support staff, local library meetings are most likely to be funded (46% and 72% respectively).

Conference Limitations

According to question thirty-two, in the majority of libraries, there is no limit to the number of conferences an individual can attend in one year. Of the eleven comments appended to this question, eight indicated that the unwritten limiter was the amount of funding available in the travel budget in a particular year.

Distribution of Funds
(Questions 25-29)

As noted earlier, the library director is most likely to distribute travel funds (82% of 125 responses). The academic administrator was a distant second (14%) and an institution-wide committee was third (7%). Earlier studies of ARL libraries often mentioned the use of some type of travel allocation committee. This is a second point of difference between the larger ARL libraries and the college and small university libraries.

How do library directors allocate travel funds? In the majority of cases, they make decisions based on the type of activity in which the library wishes to engage (37% or 46 libraries). In thirty libraries (26%), a flat amount is allocated to each person. This is supported by the fact that twenty percent of the comments received on question eighteen indicated individuals were given a flat allocation.

For the question on preferential treatment, respondents were asked to mark all that apply. Accordingly, neither numbers nor percentages will add up to 100. Preferential treatment is given equally to individuals who will either be delivering papers/ making presentations or attending meetings that directly relate to their work responsibilities (both achieved a 63% rate). Members of committees had a slight edge over those who were chairing those committees or presiding over other conference events (60% and 58% respectively). Not unexpectedly, those who were not members of the sponsoring association and just wished to attend the event received the least preferential treatment (14%).

To be eligible for travel funds library employees do not need to meet any criteria pertaining to length of service or rank since only twelve responded to this question. That is good news for those who are just entering the profession or beginning a career as a library support staff member.

Finally, in the majority of libraries (88 or 82%), librarians are able to obtain travel advances from the library or institution. Several comments indicated that advances were only available for registration and/or airfare.

Additional Funding for Participation
(Questions 30-31)

While presenting a paper or making a presentation at a conference gains librarians preferential treatment in the allocation of funds, it garners reimbursement for development costs in only slightly more than half of the responding libraries (55%). Far fewer administrations provide developmental costs for other library professionals or support staff (38% and 36% respectively). This lack of financial support holds true for those participating as panel moderators, committee chairs, etc. Comments on this question indicated that other types of support were available. Of thirteen responses, five indicated that such preparations could be done at work and four stated that faculty development grants were available.

Sources and Frequency of Funding
(Questions 33-34)

On questions thirty-three and thirty-four, respondents were again encouraged to mark all responses that applied. Consequently, neither the numbers nor the percentages add up to 100.

Travel funds come primarily from a departmental allocation (73%) with professional development funds a distant second (35%). Institutional funds can be obtained in 28% of the libraries surveyed. In general, they are disbursed as requested in 54% of responding libraries and annually for an additional 38%.

After the Conference
(Questions 35-38)

Question thirty-five emphasizes the importance of professional development travel in the career of a librarian. Such activity is used during job evaluations at 70% (88 of 125) of the responding academic libraries. Earlier, data for question fourteen indicated that in 80% of the libraries, librarians were expected to demonstrate continuing education experiences for their annual performance evaluation. The 10% difference seen here could cover continuing education activities such as workshops.

Is the knowledge overtly shared with their colleagues upon return from a professional development activity? Overwhelmingly, the answer is no. Neither written nor oral reports are required. In total, sixteen library administrators added their comments to questions thirty-six through thirty-eight. Of those, thirteen indicated that such presentations, while not mandated, are encouraged. Five specifically mentioned written reports as preferred. Several comments seemed to indicate that librarians and staff were expected to share the information in day-to-day contact with others. This practice reflects the informal nature of the travel policies themselves.

However, it is in direct contrast to the ARL libraries which, in many cases, require recipients of travel funds to make some type of report upon their return.[27] If travelers from colleges and small universities were held more accountable upon their return, would there be more support for travel?

Sabbaticals, Study Leaves and Tuition Support (Questions 39-43)

Sabbaticals

Sabbaticals are available to librarians at 56% of the institutions surveyed. Those sabbaticals are regulated by institutional policies in 49% of the cases. Typically, they are six months in length. However, the twenty-two comments added to this question indicated that there is a wide variety in the way sabbaticals are handled. At one institution, sabbaticals were mandatory after ten years. At another library, only the director was eligible, while a third provided different sabbaticals for junior and senior faculty members. In several cases, staffing levels at the library precluded anyone from taking sabbaticals. Not surprisingly, in most instances (82%), other library professionals are ineligible for sabbaticals.

Study Leaves

Similarly, study leaves are available to librarians at 52% of the institutions surveyed and in most cases are covered by an institutional policy. Over twenty-four comments were made on returned questionnaires. One indicated that leaves were in the union contract. Several indicated that, while leaves were available, none of the librarians had ever availed themselves of this option. Probably the area in which there was the most difference was the duration of a leave of absence. That ranged from one semester to two years. At another library, the director responded that "We do have a library policy whereby each tenure track librarian accrues 8 hours per month research time. This can be banked and, with the Dean's approval, can be used in segments to work on articles [and] presentations. Some have accrued enough to add a month of research leave to their sabbaticals."

In 23% of the reporting libraries, other professionals in the library are eligible for leaves of absence. Comments often mirrored those indicated above, though fewer overall comments (13) were added.

Tuition

Are librarians and other library staff supported in their quest to obtain additional master's degrees or a doctorate? Given the emphasis on professional development, the numbers here are lower than expected. At only fifty-five libraries (44%) do librarians receive such support. An

---

[27] Blomberg and Chapman, "Survey of Travel Support Policies," 92.

interesting companion question that could have been included here would have ascertained the number of institutions at which faculty were supported in their quest for a doctoral degree.

CONCLUSIONS

The results of this survey show similarities in status and requirements for library staffs in private colleges and universities. There are also parallels in how travel funds and leaves are handled. The data indicate that, while most of the librarians at the responding institutions do not have rank or tenure, 74% have some type of faculty privilege. Library staffs, excluding students, are expected to keep current in their fields at 79% of the reporting institutions and 88% are evaluated on how well they meet this expectation via an annual review. Institutions enable librarians and other staff to meet job expectations by providing travel funding 83% of the time. Liberal release time is also provided to allow participation in professional development activities. This practice compares well with previous ARL studies which indicated the same liberality.

Few of the responding libraries have separate administrative and professional development travel budgets, in contrast to the institutions responding to the earlier ARL survey. In most cases, travel funds come from a line item within the library's budget. Ultimately, available funds are allocated at the library director's discretion. The methods most often used to distribute funds are allocation of a flat amount per person and prioritization by the type of activity in which the individual is engaged. Preferential treatment is given to individuals who are participating in conferences, meetings, etc. in a meaningful way. Only 35% of reporting institutions provide librarians with additional professional development funds from outside the library. As might be expected, librarians enjoy the widest range of travel funding and professional development options, followed by staff members, and then by other professionals. Unlike their colleagues at ARL institutions, the majority of librarians in the smaller institutions are not required to make a presentation upon their return from travel.

Written policies could provide library administrators at small academic libraries a consistent and equitable method of allocating strained or diminishing travel funds, but many have not yet developed such policies (80%). Data from this survey indicates not only a predominant reliance on unwritten travel policies, but a satisfaction with this practice as well. Many comments indicated that, due to fluctuations in budgets and other changing needs, individual libraries benefit from the flexibility unwritten guidelines provide. Others report that with a small staff, unwritten policies serve them well.

Sabbaticals are available to librarians slightly more than one half (56%) of the time. In 49% of the cases, the policy is institution-wide, not library level. Librarians are eligible for study leaves of absence at about the same rate (52%) as sabbaticals. However, less than half (44%)

receive any support for obtaining additional master's degrees. In the majority of cases, other professionals and staff are not eligible for sabbaticals or study leaves of absence.

The travel, sabbatical, and study leave policies that are included in this document are representative of the broadest and most varied of policies provided by responding institutions. Sharing these documents may provide ideas to others as they contemplate the ways in which their travel funds are currently allocated and how such allocation processes could be improved.

SELECTED BIBLIOGRAPHY

Selected Bibliography

ACRL Standards for College Libraries 2000 Edition: Staff." ACRL College Libraries Section Standards Committee, 2000 [http://www.ala.org/acrl/guides/college.html#staff].

Blomberg, Donna Pittman and Karen Chapman. "Survey of Travel Support Policies at ARL Libraries." *The Journal of Academic Librarianship* 15 (May 1989): 90-3.

Cramer, Michael D. *Travel Policies in ARL Libraries*. SPEC Kit 161. Association of Research Libraries, Washington D. C.: Office of Management Studies, 1990.

DeBoer, Kee and Wendy Culotta. "The Academic Librarian and Faculty Status in the 1980's: A Survey of the Literature." *College and Research Libraries* 48 (May 1987): 215-223.

English, Thomas G. "Librarian Status in the Eighty-Nine U.S. Academic Institutions of the Association of Research Libraries: 1982." *College and Research Libraries* 44 (May 1983): 199-211.

Kingma, Bruce R. and Gillian M. McCombs. "The Opportunity Costs of Faculty Status for Academic Librarians." *College & Research Libraries* 56 (May 1995): 258-64.

Kratz, Charles E. and Valerie A. Platz. *The Personnel Manual: An Outline for Libraries*. 2nd ed. Chicago: American Library Association, 1993.

"Libraries Polled On Travel Policies." *College and Research Libraries News* 41 (July/August 1980): 195-196.

Morein, P. Grady. "What is a CLIP Note?" *College and Research Libraries News* 46 (May 1985): 226.

Phillips, Jen. "Travel Policies – replies." Online posting. 12 February 2001. COLLIB-L@acs.wooster.edu.

Professional Development in ARL Libraries / Systems and Procedures Exchange Center. SPEC Kit 86. Washington D. C.: Office of Management Studies, Association of Research Libraries, 1982. [Note: Updates SPEC Kit no. 51 (1979)].

Professional Development in ARL Libraries / Systems and Procedures Exchange Center. SPEC Kit 51. Washington D. C.: Office of Management Services, Association of Research Libraries, 1979.

Rai, Priya. "Summary of Benefits Survey." Online posting. 16 March 2000. COLLIB-L@acs.wooster.edu.

Ring, Daniel F. "Professional Development Leave As A Stepping Stone to Faculty Status." *The Journal of Academic Librarianship* 4 (March 1978): 19-20.

Travel Program 1999/2000. Library, University of California, Berkeley. Librarians Association of the University of California. LAUC-B Travel Program, 1999/2000. Http://www.lib.berkeley.edu/LAUC/travel.html.

Travel Policies of Twenty-One College and University Libraries. Chicago: Association of College and Research Libraries, 1980.

Vesper, Virginia and Gloria Kelley, comps. *Criteria for Promotion and Tenure for Academic Librarians.* CLIP Note #26. College Library Information Packet Committee, College Libraries Section, Association of College and Research Libraries, a Division of the American Library Association. Chicago, 1997.

Wilding, Thomas L. "Career and staff development: A convergence." *C & R L News* 50 (November 1989): 899-902.

Wright, James. "Fringe Benefits for Academic Library Personnel." *College and Research Libraries* 31 (January 1970): 18-21.

Yao, Winberta, "Travel Funds Committees." *College and Research Libraries News* 41 (December 1980): 330.

CLIP NOTE SURVEY RESULTS

ASSOCIATION OF COLLEGE AND RESEARCH LIBRARIES
COLLEGE LIBRARY SECTION/CLIP NOTE QUESTIONNAIRE
TRAVEL, SABBATICAL, AND STUDY LEAVE POLICIES FOR
PROFESSIONAL DEVELOPMENT

This survey document is designed to gather information about travel and sabbatical policies in academic libraries.

INSTITUTIONAL INFORMATION

Date_____

Institution Name _____

Library Name _____

Institution Status: Public *99 (79%)   Private *26 (21%)*

Address _____

_____

Name of Respondent _____

Position Title _____

Work Telephone_____

E-mail Address _____

Fax _____

ALL FIGURES SHOULD BE FOR FISCAL YEAR 1998-1999. REQUESTED STATISTICS SHOULD BE BASED ON IPEDS CATEGORIES AND DEFINITIONS.

INSTITUTIONAL INFORMATION

1. Number of full-time equivalent (FTE) students
   118 responses   *2,411 average*   *1,936 median*

2. Number of full-time equivalent (FTE) faculty
   116 responses   *155 average*   *128 median*

3. Number of full-time equivalent (FTE) librarians
   123 responses   *7 average*   *6 median*

4. Number of other full-time equivalent (FTE) professionals
   100 responses   *5 average*   *1.8 median*

5. Number of all other full-time equivalent (FTE) paid staff
    119 responses   *15 average*   *7.8 median*

6. Number of full-time equivalent (FTE) student assistants
    121 responses   *9 average*   *7.3 median*

7. Total full-time equivalent (FTE) staff (sum lines 3 - 6)
    120 responses   *28 average*   *20 median*

8. Total Materials Expenditure
    17 responses   *$508,293 average*   *$343,582 median*

9. Total professional travel expenditures, if paid from library budget
    101 responses   *$6,197 average*   *$3,500 median*

    The highest amount expended for travel was $21,684; the lowest was $80.

Over $20,000	*4 responses*	*(4%)*
$15,000 - $20,000	*5 responses*	*(5%)*
$10,000 - $15,000	*16 responses*	*(16%)*
$5,000 - $10,000	*22 responses*	*(22%)*
1,000 - $5,000	*2 responses*	*(42%)*
Under $1,000	*2 responses*	*(12%)*

10. Total administrative travel expenditures
    44 responses   *$2,740 average*   *2,000 median*

11. Total Expenditures (include fringe benefits if paid from library budget)
    93 responses   *$1,171,607 average*

RANK AND TENURE STATUS

12. Check the following as it applies to your librarians (i.e. ALA accredited degree).
    Respondents were asked to mark all that applied, resulting in percentages over 100.

    faculty status (implies having the same responsibilities and privileges as teaching faculty).
    56 responses   *45 %*

    academic rank (Holds title of instructor, assistant, associate or full professor or equivalent)
    37 responses   *30%*

    academic status (Librarians share some faculty privileges)
    28 responses   *22%*

    administrative status
    34 responses   *27%*

staff status
13 responses   *10%*

other, please specify:
1 response   *1%*

13. Check the following as it applies to <u>other professional</u> staff (i.e. holding other masters or doctorate degrees).

faculty status (Faculty status implies the acceptance of the same responsibilities and privileges as teaching faculty).
2 responses   *3%*

academic rank (Holds title of instructor, assistant, associate or full professor or equivalent)
3 responses   *4%*

academic status (Share some faculty privileges)
5 responses   *6%*

administrative status
37 responses   *47%*

staff status
28 responses   *36%*

other, please specify:
3 responses   *4%*

CONTINUING EDUCATION SECTION

14. Are staff required to remain current in their fields?

librarians
120 responses   *100 yes (83%)*   *20 no (17%)*

other professionals
78 responses   *56 yes (72%)*   *22 no (28%)*

non-professional staff
112 responses   *64 yes (57%)*   *48 no(43%)*

a. If yes, is demonstration of such continuing education required for:

promotion
   librarians
     93 responses   *67 yes (72%)*   *26 no (28%)*

other professionals
57 responses   **12 yes (21%)**   **45 no (79%)**

non-professional staff
78 responses   **10 yes (13%)**   **68 no (87%)**

tenure
librarians
78 responses   **37 yes (47%)**   **41 no (53%)**

other professionals
50 responses   **3 yes (6%)**   **47 no (94%)**

on-professional staff
63 responses   **0 yes (0%)**   **3 no (100%)**

annual performance evaluation
librarian
104 responses   **92 yes (88%)**   **12 no (12%)**

other professionals
70 responses   **51 yes (73%)**   **19 no (27%)**

non-professional staff
100 responses   **62 yes (62%)**   **38 no (38%)**

15. Does a union contract govern (check all that apply)? If no, go to next question.

promotion
librarians
10 responses   **9 yes (90%)**   **1 no (10%)**

other professionals
4 responses   **4 yes (100%)**   **0 no (0%)**

staff
6 responses   **6 yes (100%)**   **0 no (0%)**

tenure
librarians

9 responses   **9 yes (100%)**   **0 no (0%)**

other professionals
4 responses   **3 yes (75%)**   **1 no (25%)**

staff
5 responses   **4 yes (80%)**   **1 no (20%)**

performance review

     librarians
     10 responses   *10 yes (100%)*   *0 no (0%)*

     other professionals
     7 responses   *7 yes (100%)*   *0 no (0%)*

     staff
     12 responses   *12 yes (100%)*   *0 no (0%)*

travel

     librarians
     1 response   *1 yes (100%)*   *0 no (0%)*

     other professionals
     0 responses   *0 yes (0%)*   *0 no (0%)*

     staff
     1 response   *1 yes (100%)*   *0 no (0%)*

PROFESSIONAL DEVELOPMENT TRAVEL SECTION

16. Does your <u>institution</u> have a formal, written, campus-wide travel policy that provides institutional level funds for:

     librarians
     125 responses   *45 yes (36%)*   *80 no (64%)*

     other professionals
     94 responses   *26 yes (28%)*   *68 no (72%)*

     non-professional staff
     114 responses   *20 yes (18%)*   *94 no (82%)*

  a. If yes, does it cover travel to international meetings, conventions, etc.?

     librarians
     56 responses   *38 yes (68%)*   *18 no (32%)*

     other professionals
     40 responses   *20 yes (50%)*   *20 no (50%)*

     non-professional staff
     47 responses   *9 yes (19%)*   *38 no (81%)*

  b. If yes, does it provide funds to supplement the library's travel fund

     librarians
     50 responses   *30 yes (60%)*   *20 no (40%)*

other professionals
34 responses   **11 yes (32%)**   **23 no (68%)**

non-professional staff
42 responses   **6 yes (14%)**   **36 no (86%)**

17. Has your <u>library</u> developed a formal, written, travel policy that provides library budget level funds for:

librarians
    121 response   **9 yes (7%)**   **112 no (93%)**

other professionals
    92 responses   **7 yes (8%)**   **85 no (92%)**

non-professional staff
    118 responses   **12 yes (10%)**   **106 no (90%)**

a. If yes, is it based on a campus-wide institution policy?

librarians
    15 responses   **1 yes (7%)**   **14 no (93%)**

other professionals
    13 responses   **1 yes (8%)**   **12 no (92%)**

non-professional staff
    16 responses   **1 yes (6%)**   **15 no (94%)**

18. Does your <u>library</u> have an informal, **unwritten**, library budget **level** travel policy that covers:

librarians
    120 responses   **96 yes (80%)**   **24 no (20%)**

other professionals
    72 responses   **50 yes (69%)**   **22 no (31%)**

non-professional staff
    107 responses   **80 yes (75%)**   **27 no (25%)**

a. If yes, please provide a brief description of the policy:

b. If yes, is it based on a campus-wide institution policy?

librarians
86 responses   **17 yes (20%)**   **69 no (80%)**

other professionals
55 responses   **11 yes (20%)**   **44 no (80%)**

non-professional staff
76 responses   **11 yes (14%)**   **65 no (86%)**

19. Does the <u>library</u> have an administrative travel budget, separate from its professional development travel budget, which allows library directors or other library administrators to conduct library business?
24 responses   **26 yes (21%)**   **98 no (79%)**

20. Does the<u> institution</u> have a separate administrative travel budget which provides funds to library directors or other library administrators to enable them to conduct library business?
121 responses   **18 yes (15%)**   **103 no(85%)**

21. If your library does not have a formal or informal travel policy, please briefly identify the reason(s).

IF YOUR LIBRARY/INSTITUTION HAS A TRAVEL POLICY, PLEASE CONTINUE

22. What elements does the travel policy cover? Mark all that apply.

a. Librarians   Other Professionals Staff

94 (75%)	**49 (39%)**	**76 (61%)**	Registration fees
88 (70%)	**43 (34%)**	**56 (45%)**	Air fare
82 (66%)	**41 (33%)**	**50 (40%)**	Travel to/from airport
93 (74%)	**46 (37%)**	**64 (51%)**	Lodging costs
83 (66%)	**42 (34%)**	**63 (50%)**	Per Diem (i.e. meals, etc.)
93 (74%)	**48 (38%)**	**71 (57%)**	Mileage when own car is used
78 (62%)	**39 (31%)**	**52 (42%)**	Rental vehicle, if necessary
			Other, please specify:

b. This is policy is:

institutional level   **36 (29%)**
library level   **58 (46%)**
both   **29 (23%)**

23. For what purposes are the travel funds allocated?

National library association conventions, conferences, meetings, etc.

106 (85%)	librarians
37 (30%)	other professionals
32 (26%)	non-professional staff

Regional library association conventions, conferences, meetings, etc.

105 (84%)	librarians
51 (41%)	other professionals
71 (57%)	non-professional staff

National pre-conferences to library association conventions, conferences, meetings, etc.

96 (77%)	librarians
37 (30%)	other professionals
27 (22%)	non-professional staff

Regional pre-conferences to library association conventions, conferences, meetings, etc.

98 (78 %)	librarians
45 (36%)	other professionals
55 (44%)	non-professional staff

National related professional conventions, conferences, etc.

94 (75%)	librarians
40 (32%)	other professionals
26 (21%)	non-professional staff

Regional related professional conventions, conferences, etc.

94 (75%)	librarians
44 (35%)	other professionals
57 (46%)	non-professional staff

Regional pre-conferences to related professional conventions, conferences, etc.

80 (64%)	librarians
39 (31%)	other professionals
49 (39%)	non-professional staff

National pre-conferences to related professional conventions or conferences

76 (61%)	librarians
35 (28%)	other professionals
23 (18%)	non-professional staff

Committee meetings for national associations
- *79 (63%)*   librarians
- *33 (26%)*   other professionals
- *18 (14%)*   non-professional staff

Committee meetings for regional associations
- *98 (78%)*   librarians
- *46 (37%)*   other professionals
- *53 (42%)*   non-professional staff

Local library related meetings of any type
- *101 (81%)*   librarians
- *57 (46%)*   other professionals
- *90 (72%)*   non-professional staff

Taking local or regional library related classes:
- *73 (58%)*   librarians
- *40 (32%)*   other professionals
- *63 (50%)*   non-professional staff

All of the above
- *38 (30%)*   librarians
- *16 (13%)*   other professionals
- *12 (10%)*   non-professional staff

Other, please specify:

24. Who determines distribution of funds?

library director	*102 (82%)*
library travel committee	*2 (2%)*
other library committee	*2 (2%)*
institutional-wide committee	*9 (9%)*
Academic Dean, Vice-President for Academic Admin. etc.	*18 (14%)*
Other	*2 (2%)*

25. How are funds allocated? Mark all that apply.

% of total cost	*19 (15%)*
flat amount per person	*33 (26%)*
matching basis	*1 (1%)*
formula for dividing funds among staff	*12 (10%)*
rank (professor, associate professor, etc.)	*3 (2%)*
type of meeting, workshop, convention, etc.	*46 (37%)*

level of tenure	2 (2%)
other, please specify:	2 (2%)

26. Are any of the following used for identifying preferential order of personnel selection for travel funds? (Mark all that apply).

library representation at meeting, convention, workshop, etc.	63 (50%)
delivery of papers/presentations	79 (63%)
officer, chair, presides over meetings, etc.	72 (58%)
members of committees meeting at conference, panel member, etc.	75 (60%)
attendee only, members of sponsoring association, society, etc.	28 (22%)
attendee only, non-member of sponsoring association, society, etc.	18 (14%)
value to library through meetings that relate directly to a person's work responsibilities	46 (37%)

27. Do eligibility rules apply such as (mark all that apply):

must have worked for library/institution for one year or more	4 (3%)
must have worked for the library/institution 6 months or more	6 (5%)
must have tenure	0 (0%)
must have attained rank of assistant professor (or equivalent) or higher	2 (2%)

28. Are travel advances allowed?

107 responses   *88 yes (70%)*   *19 no (18%)*

29. Does library/institution provide reimbursement for developmental costs for preparing a presentation?

librarians
98 responses   *54 yes (55%)*   *44 no (45%)*

other professionals
61 responses   *23 yes (38%)*   *38 no (62%)*

non-professional staff
67 responses   *24 yes (36%)*   *43 no (64%)*

30. Does the institution provide additional funds for participation such as panel moderator, chair of committee/section, meeting coordinator, officer of organization, etc.

105 responses   *23 yes (22%)*   *82 no (78%)*

31. Is there a limit to the number of conferences:

a librarian may attend
101 responses   *28 yes (28%)*   *73 no (72%)*

other professional staff may attend
66 responses   *21 yes (32%)*   *45 no (68%)*

a non-professional staff member may attend
93 responses   *29 yes (31%)*   *64 no (69%)*

32. How frequently are travel funds allocated?

quarterly	*1 (1%)*
semi-annually	*1 (1%)*
annually	*48 (38%)*
as requested	*68 (54%)*
other, please specify	*0 (0%)*

33. From what source(s) do the travel funds come? (Mark all that apply).

department allocation	*91 (73%)*
institutional travel budget	*35 (28%)*
recruitment funds	*3 (2%)*
professional development funds	*44 (35%)*
endowment funds	*8 (6%)*
other, please specify	*17 (14%)*

34. How is the attendance and/or presentation of papers at professional association meetings utilized (Mark all that apply)?

job performance evaluation	*88 (70%)*
tenure/continuing employment	*45 (36%)*
advancement in rank	*51 (41%)*

35. Is a presentation to library staff required?

librarians
105 responses   *22 yes (21%)*   *83 no (79%)*

other professionals
68 responses   *4 yes (6%)*   *64 no (94%)*

non-professional staff
94 responses   *8 yes (9%)*   *86 no (91%)*

36. Is a presentation to the campus community required afterwards?

  librarians
  107 responses   *1 yes (1%)*   *106 no (99%)*

  other professionals
  71 responses   *0 yes (0%)*   *1 no (100%)*

  non-professional staff
  98 responses   *0 yes (0%)*   *98 no (100%)*

37. Is a written report required upon return from travel?

  librarians
  107 responses   *21 yes (20%)*   *86 no (80%)*

  other professionals
  67 responses   *8 yes (12%)*   *59 no (88%)*

  non-professional staff
  96 responses   *12 yes (13%)*   *84 no (87%)*

SABBATICALS AND STUDY LEAVES

38. Are the librarians at your institution eligible for sabbaticals? *(Sabbaticals are leaves for such activities as planned programs of research, writing, or travel).*

  123 responses   *69 yes (56%)*   *54 no (44%)*

 a. If yes, is the policy (mark all that apply):

institutional level	*61 responses*	*61 yes (100%)*	*0 no (0%)*
library level policy	*3 responses*	*3 yes (100%)*	*0 no (0%)*
both	*2 responses*	*2 yes (100%)*	*0 no (0%)*
union contract	*10 responses*	*10 yes (100%)*	*0 no (0%)*
other, specify:	*0 responses*	*0 yes (0%)*	*0 no (0%)*

 b. If yes, how long is a typical leave?

3 months	*15 responses*
6 months	*26 responses*
9 months	*7 responses*
other, please specify:	

  Please attach policy and/or forms or describe process for obtaining a sabbatical.

39. Are the other professionals at your library eligible for sabbaticals? *(Sabbaticals are generally paid leaves for such activities as planned programs of research, writing, or travel).*

  90 responses   *16 yes (18%)*   *74 no (82%)*

a. If yes, is the policy:

institutional level	*12 responses*	*12 yes (100%)*	*0 no (0%)*
library level	*0 responses*	*0 yes (0%)*	*0 no (0%)*
both	*0 responses*	*0 yes (0%)*	*0 no (0%)*
union contract	*2 responses*	*2 yes (100%)*	*0 no (0%)*
other, specify:	*0 responses*	*0 yes (0%)*	*0 no (0%)*

b. If yes, how long is a typical leave?

3 months	*2 responses*
6 months	*8 responses*
9 months	*0 responses*
other, specify:	*0 responses*

Please attach policies and/or describe process for obtaining a sabbatical.

40. Are the librarians at your institution eligible for study leaves of absence? *(Leaves of absence can be paid or unpaid and generally cover graduate study leave or extensive research projects).*

   121 responses   *63 yes (52%)*   *58 no (48%)*

a. If yes, is the policy:

institutional level	*45 responses*	*42 yes (93%)*	*3 no (7%)*
library level	*3 responses*	*3 yes (100%)*	*0 no (0%)*
both	*2 responses*	*2 yes (100%)*	*0 no (0%)*

b. If yes, how long is a typical leave?

3 months	*9 responses*	*9 yes (100%)*	*0 no (0%)*
6 months	*6 responses*	*6 yes (100%)*	*0 no (0%)*
9 months	*8 responses*	*8 yes (100%)*	*0 no (0%)*
other, please specify:	*27 responses*	*2 yes (7%)*	*25 no (93%)*

Please provide policy or briefly describe process for obtaining study leave

41. Are the other professionals at your library eligible for study leaves of absence? *(Leaves of absence can be paid or unpaid and generally cover graduate study leave or extensive research projects).*

   85 responses   *23 yes (27%)*   *62 no (73%)*

a. If yes, is the policy:

institutional level	*13 responses*	*13 yes (100%)*	*0 no (0%)*
library level	*0 responses*	*0 yes (0%)*	*0 no (0%)*
both	*0 responses*	*0 yes (0%)*	*0 no (0%)*

b. If yes, how long is a typical leave?

3 months	*6 responses*	*6 yes (100%)*	*0 no (0%)*
6 months	*4 responses*	*4 yes (100%)*	*0 no (0%)*
9 months	*2 responses*	*2 yes (100%)*	*0 no (0%)*
other, specify:	*6 responses*	*6 yes (100%)*	*0 no (0%)*

Please provide policy or briefly describe process for obtaining study leave.

42. Are the librarians at your institution eligible for tuition support for continuing education (i.e. obtaining additional master's or Ph.D. degrees)?

116 responses　　*55 yes (47%)*　　*61 no (53%)*

If yes, is the policy:

institutional level	*45 responses*	*45 yes (100%)*	*0 no (0%)*
library level policy	*1 responses*	*1 yes (100%)*	*0 no (0%)*
other	*1 responses*	*1 yes (100%)*	*0 no (0%)*

TRAVEL, SABBATICAL, AND STUDY LEAVE POLICIES

General Travel Policies

Albion College
Albion, Michigan

Allentown College
(DeSales University)
Allentown, Pennsylvania

Drew University
Madison, New Jersey

Mary Washington College
Fredericksburg, Virginia

Messiah College
Grantham, Pennsylvania

Middlebury College
Middlebury, Vermont

Oberlin College
Oberlin, Ohio

Providence College
Providence, Rhode Island

Saint Olaf College
Northfield, Minnesota

Southwest Baptist University
Bolivar, Missouri

University of the South
Sewanee, Tennessee

William Patterson University of New Jersey
Wayne, New Jersey

STOCKWELL-MUDD STAFF DEVELOPMENT AND TRAVEL POLICY

One of the goals of the Albion College Library program is support for staff development. Staff development includes attendance at internal and external workshops, classes, and meetings that develop and/or improve the skills, information, and knowledge of staff members in performing their assigned job responsibilities. All staff members are encouraged and, in some cases, required to attend development programs. The primary intent of a staff development program is staff improvement for better library services.

All regular library staff are expected to take advantage of job related development programs. This includes programs that focus on job skills, time management skills, interpersonal skills, or other skills that improve work performance or productivity. Programs sponsored by various offices on campus or offered by such organizations as the Woodlands Library Cooperative, Michigan Library Consortium, Library of Michigan, Michigan Library Association, or by a contracted service agency are eligible for support by the Library.

Librarians are expected to be professionally active through membership in appropriate organizations and through attendance at professional meetings. They are also encouraged to participate in appropriate professional organizations as committee members, as officers, or as program presenters. The Library supports attendance by librarians to the extent conference and travel funds are available. Requests for funds to attend professional meetings must be approved by the Director of Libraries.

Support is provided according to the following priority:

1. Any approved in-state workshop and training program sponsored by MLC, MLA, Library of Michigan, Woodlands Library Cooperative, or other approved professional organization.
2. National and regional professional meetings sponsored by ALA, ACRL, Oberlin Group, LOEX, MFLA, Library of Congress, Innovative Interfaces Inc., NASIG, GPO Depository Program, EDUCOM, CLAC, or other recognized professional organizations that might be added to this list.

The library supports in full an official representative to the following meetings:

- At least one representative to the Winter and Summer conferences of the American Library Association.
- At least one representative to the periodic meetings of ACRL.
- The Library Director to attend the annual meetings of the Oberlin Group.

In addition, the library will support all librarians attending the MLA annual conference. Support will also be provided, to the extent funds are available, for librarians desiring to attend conferences and meetings of other sanctioned organizations listed above.

3.23 TRAVEL POLICY

All travel on College business is to be approved in advance by the administrator with budget responsibility. The travel policy does not pertain to personal travel during the day or travel to or from work. For travel on College business, the most direct route and the most economical method of transportation should be used.

If you utilize your personal vehicle on College business you will be reimbursed at the established College mileage rate, plus any tolls and/or parking expenses. Reimbursed mileage will be either from your place of residence or the College, whichever is the shortest distance.

Ordinarily, you may obtain a travel advance from the Treasurer's Office, provided the requisition is received in that office at least five days prior to your departure, or you may have expenses reimbursed after the trip has been completed. In either case, you must complete a Travel Voucher Form at the conclusion of the trip. The Treasurer's Office is prepared to handle either a travel advance or a travel reimbursement by means of petty cash if the amount is less than $75.00

DREW UNIVERSITY LIBRARY

POLICY ON PROFESSIONAL MEETINGS, TRAVEL, AND REIMBURSEMENT FOR LIBRARY FACULTY

INTRODUCTION

The involvement of Drew's library faculty in professional organizations and other activities is an integral and important part of our professional life. The library supports such activity by providing released time and nominal financial support. Released time for attendance at meetings is a privilege, the granting of which is rarely questioned. Financial support, unfortunately, is less available.

Rather than create a hierarchy of professional activities, the library faculty asserts the principle that it is important that we each contribute to the profession as our specific library positions and personal interests incline, thereby enriching our service to Drew University. For Drew, of course, it is important that we be represented at ATLA, but it is also important that we have librarians involved in ALA, ACRL, NJLA and other groups, state- and nation-wide, identified as professionally relevant to our library faculty, library, or university.

Every librarian should consider that a small portion of the travel budget exists to support his/her professional travel costs, although our levels of activity and related costs vary. The Committee on Faculty will provide guidance to the library administration in determining what professional priorities to support among the various options available to the faculty in a given period.

The following guidelines, developed and approved by the library faculty in 1979, and slightly amended in 1983, remain essentially valid. As costs and inflation have risen, however, the size of the travel budget has remained unchanged. Hence the suggested figures cannot always be met, some of the guidelines are more ideal than real, and the administration of the budget is necessarily flexible.

POLICY

Attendance at and participation in professional and scholarly meetings and seminars is an appropriate use of part of library faculty member's time and effort. To encourge this activity, the library will support library faculty participation in professional associations by providing released time and some monetary reimbursement as budget and guidelines permit.

Every member of the library faculty is eligible to apply for a travel allotment to help finance his or her attendance at professional meetings.

The travel budget will be administered by the library administration with the advice of the Library Committee on Faculty.

Each faculty member is eligible for one travel grant during the fiscal year (July 1 - June 30). A second grant may be considered when the faculty member is included on the official program of the meeting as an officer, speaker or committee member and funds are available.

Faculty members should be members of the organization whose meeting they plan to attend or the program should be one that is relevant to the needs of the library.

rev. 7/86

DREW UNIVERSITY LIBRARY

POLICY FOR DISTRIBUTION OF LIBRARY FACULTY FUNDS FOR SCHOLARLY PROJECTS

PURPOSE: The Library will make limited funds available for support of scholarly projects, particularly those leading to publication.   Applicants must be librarians with clearly defined projects in an area of academic interest. Funds may be used for expenses such as the following:

> typing of manuscripts
> photocopying of materials not readily accessible
> travel to libraries and research collections
> student research assistants
> copyright fees
> software specifically tailored to a research project
> supplementing matching grants

AMOUNT: Librarians may apply between July and May of the fiscal year in advance of anticipated expenses up to a request of $100, and may apply for additional funding until June 15 for expenses incurred. Normally no librarian will be granted more than $300 per year. If the budget has been exhausted for the year, librarians may make requests in the following year for expenses incurred.   It is the responsibility of the Library Committee on Faculty to notify librarians of available funds in the current and projected budgets in May of each year.

PROCEDURE: Requests should be made to the Library Committee on Faculty, and allocations will be made by the Director in consultation with the Committee. Requests should contain a description of the project, plans for publication, a detailed list of projected expenses, and receipts or other documentation for actual expenses. Librarians who have received advance funding should submit a documented account of expenses for which the grant was used. Applications for funding of multi-year projects must be submitted each year.

PROFITS: Should a librarian gain financially from the project, funds provided by the Library should be returned.

Approved by the Library Faculty, November 4, 1985

MARY WASHINGTON COLLEGE

TRAVEL AND BUSINESS MEAL POLICIES AND PROCEDURES

CONTENTS:

- Applicability
- Travel Planning
- Travel Expense Reimbursement
- Required Documentation For Reimbursement
- Lodging
- Meals and Incidental Travel Expenses
- Allowable/Unallowable Miscellaneous Expenses
- Personally-Owned Transportation
- Mileage Reimbursement Rates
- Attendance at an Event By More Than 2 College Employees
- Travel Cash Advances
- Business Meals
- Team and Club Travel
- Air and Rail Travel
- Reimbursement and Time Frames

APPENDIX:

- **List of Senior Staff Members**
- **"Request For Overnight Professional Travel" Form**
- **"Travel Expense Reimbursement Voucher" Form**
- **Lodging and Meals and Incidental Expense Table**
- **"Use of State Vehicle" form: Page 1   Page 2**
- **"Request For Temporary Advance" Form**
- **"Business Meal/Use of College Credit Card" Form**
- **Business Meal Allowable Rates**
- **Mileage Reimbursement Rates (bottom of this page)**
- **New Travel Agency Contract Procedures**
- **Dept. of Accounts Meal and Lodging Rate Tables Section 20300, pg 17, 18**
- **Foreign Currency Exchange Rates**

APPLICABILITY

These procedures specifically apply to all MWC Departments and Offices. They are based on the Commonwealth of Virginia Accounting Policies and Procedures Manual, Topic 20335, State Travel Regulations, which is the final authority where conflicts with College policies occur.

Departments and offices within the College may adopt more restrictive policies and procedures as approved by the respective Senior Staff Member. A listing of Senior Staff Members with approval authority is included in the Appendix. Some older forms may still refer to "Cabinet Member" or "Executive Committee". These terms should be interpreted to mean "Senior Staff". These procedures also apply to guests of the College such as speakers, job candidates and others for whom the College is responsible for expense reimbursement.

TRAVEL PLANNING

Utilizing the "Request for Overnight Professional Travel," provide written cost estimates, prior to traveling, for all overnight travel. Costs include lodging, meals, transportation, registration and course fees. The appropriate department head or budget manager and Senior Staff Member or his/her designee must approve the request.

Out-of-Country travel also requires prior written approval and in addition, must be approved by the President or his designee, the Executive Vice President. This form must be submitted with the Travel Reimbursement Voucher when requesting reimbursement.

TRAVEL EXPENSE REIMBURSEMENT

The "Travel Expense Reimbursement Voucher" is the authorized document for requesting reimbursement of travel expenses. It, along with bills and receipts as required, provides support for reimbursement. This State form is available through the Accounts Payable/Disbursing Office in Brent Hall. Offices may request a supply of such forms to maintain on site.

REQUIRED DOCUMENTATION FOR REIMBURSEMENT

The following information is required for expense reimbursement and must be maintained and provided by the traveler:

- Purpose of travel and traveler's social security number on "Travel Expense Reimbursement Voucher"
- **Original** itemized receipt for lodging, reflecting balance paid in full
- Receipts for registration fees
- Receipts for public transportation expenses (i.e., taxi, shuttle, bus, rail, plane ticket receipts)
- Special approvals, including but not limited to overnight and out of country travel ("Request for Overnight Professional Travel" form)
- Receipts for tolls and parking when costs for any one item exceeds $10

LODGING

The maximum expenditure rates for lodging are established annually by the Commonwealth. The rates are provided on a city by city basis in a table included with these procedures. The maximum reimbursable rates exclude local taxes and surcharges which may be added and which are reimbursable to the traveler.

Lodging expenses incurred beyond these maximum rates will not be reimbursed. In such instances, local taxes and surcharges will be pro-rated based on the maximum allowable rate.

Exception: The appropriate Senior Staff Member may approve reimbursement for lodging up to

150% of the maximum rate when circumstances warrant. This approval must be so noted on the "Request for Overnight Professional Travel" form.

Original, itemized hotel bills reflecting balance paid in full are required for reimbursement.

Direct agency billing of lodging expenses is permitted and encouraged. Many lodging establishments will accept Purchase Orders from MWC and direct bill the College. Contact the Purchasing Office (654-1057) for details. All necessary approvals as outlined above, must be secured.

MEALS AND INCIDENTAL TRAVEL EXPENSES (M & I E)

Meals and certain other travel expenses (incidentals) are reimbursable for overnight official business travel outside the traveler's official station. Incidental expenses include bellhop, taxi and shuttle tips, personal telephone calls, laundry, travel between lodging and places where meals are taken, and other individual needs.

Maximum meal and incidental rates are issued by the Commonwealth. The most recent table outlining those rates is included in the Appendix. As with lodging, the maximum per diem rates are based on location (city or county). Also included with this table is a breakdown of per meal (breakfast, lunch, dinner) maximum rates.

On a travel departure or return day, 75% of the per diem is allowable based on:

- departure day - where you spend the night
- return day - where you spent the night before returning home.

When meals are provided at no cost to the traveler, such as in conjunction with a conference, the per diem rate is reduced by the allowable rate for that meal. However, when meals are provided at no cost in conjunction with an event, on a travel departure or return day, the full per diem is reduced by the full amount of the appropriate meals, followed by a 75% prorating of the balance. For example, at a Richmond meeting, breakfast is provided at no cost on the day the traveler is returning home. Calculation of the per diem is as follows: ($42 - $9) x 75% = $24.75.

ALLOWABLE MISCELLANEOUS EXPENSES

- Taxes and surcharges for lodging
- Business telephone calls, telegrams, faxes
- Parking Fees
- Road Tolls

UNALLOWABLE MISCELLANEOUS EXPENSES

- Lost or stolen articles
- Alcoholic beverages
- Damage to personal vehicle or items

- Movies charged to hotel bills
- Fines and other expenses related to personal negligence
- Entertainment expenses
- Towing charges for personal vehicle
- Charges for spouse, children and companions
- Personal needs such as medication, refrigeration, hotel safe or other conveniences.

PERSONALLY-OWNED TRANSPORTATION

Employees are permitted to use their personal vehicles when a State vehicle is not available. State vehicles can be secured through the College's transportation office in Facilities Services, using a "Request for the Use of a State Vehicle" form, which is included in the Appendix. Personal vehicles may also be used if it is beneficial to the College to do so, such as when a car is to be left at the airport for an extended period or when round-trip mileage is less than 100 miles. Employees electing to use their personal vehicle as a matter of preference or convenience will be reimbursed at a reduced rate.

MILEAGE REIMBURSEMENT RATES

Rates are outlined in the attached table included in the Appendix.

AUTOMOBILE RENTAL

When necessary and approved, employees may rent an automobile for use in conducting State business. The Commonwealth carries the necessary insurances so no additional coverage needs to be purchased. All fuel for the automobile must be purchased from service stations as opposed to the rental company which often charge a premium for refueling. Costs associated with additional insurance and refueling charges as outlined above, are not reimbursable.

TRAVEL CASH ADVANCES

The Commonwealth and College discourage the use of cash advances, however, when approved by a Senior Staff Member at the College, the following procedures apply.

The traveler completes a "Request For Temporary Advance" form, obtaining the necessary approval and signatures, and forwards the form to the Accounts Payable/Disbursing Office in Brent Hall at least 6 working days before the money is needed. Within five (5) working days of the receipt of the advance request in the Accounts Payable/Disbursing Office, a check is cut and delivered to the Cashier in G. W. Hall. The traveler visits the Cashier, signs the form acknowledging receipt of the check and receives the check. The cash advance may be received by the traveler no more than ten (10) working days prior to departure. $200 is the minimum amount which may be requested in a cash advance.

The traveler is reimbursed for all allowable trip expenses as documented on the Travel Expense Reimbursement Voucher and then must deliver a personal check to the Cashier reimbursing the College for the advance within 30 calendar days of receipt of the advance. The advance should be noted but not deducted on the Travel Expense Reimbursement Voucher.

Specific offices or departments in the College may also be eligible for permanent advances. Please see the appropriate Senior Staff Member for details.

BUSINESS MEALS

Generally, meal expenses that do not involve an overnight stay are not reimbursable. The exception involves Business Meals.

Business Meals are reimbursable expenses when:

- The appropriate Senior Staff member approves.
- It involves a substantive and bona-fide business discussion.
- An original and detailed receipt for the meal is provided.
- A list by name of all persons involved in the meal and the reason for the meal is provided.
- A completed "Business Meal/Use of College Credit Card" form is completed in advance.
- Alcoholic beverages are not included in the reimbursement request.

The College member may be reimbursed based on the rates outlined in the Business Meal Reimbursement Table included in the Appendix.

The Executive Vice President's Office maintains several College credit cards which may be utilized for business meals only. Faculty and staff are encouraged to take advantage of this option. A call or e-mail to the Executive Vice President's secretary (654-1020) will start this very simple and convenient process. The same "Business Meal/Use of College Credit Card" form is utilized here also.

TEAM AND CLUB TRAVEL

Expenses incurred by faculty, staff and students for athletic team travel and club travel may be reimbursed, when applicable, utilizing the "Travel Expense Reimbursement Voucher" and following the same procedures outlined in this document. Intercollegiate athletic team travel utilizes IFAS (Integrated Fund Accounting System) on-line requests for travel advances and reimbursements.

AIR AND RAIL TRAVEL

The College contracts on an annual basis for optional travel management services (i.e., a travel agency's services). This means that travelers on official college business may elect whether or not to use the contracted travel agency. The firm holding the contract will make reservations, assist in planning and will bill the College. Faculty and staff are to call the travel agency directly to make arrangements. If faculty and staff choose to make travel arrangements using other means, the procedures outlined in the Travel Services Contract Administrator's 10/27/98 Memorandum must be followed. For more details, call the College contract administrator (654-1234) or the Purchasing Office (654-1057).

REIMBURSEMENT TIME FRAMES

The Accounts Payable/Disbursing Office will attempt whenever possible, to process and direct that a check be sent to a faculty or staff member, or student, within five (5) working days of receipt of complete and correct reimbursement or cash advance documentation.

Generally, travel reimbursement requests received after June 15 will be charged to the next fiscal year budget (which begins July 1). There may be circumstances in some years which preclude adherence to this date.

The traveler's supervisor must approve and sign the traveler's Travel Expense Reimbursement Voucher within 3 working days of receiving it from the traveler. Travel Expense Reimbursement Voucher's must also reflect the account code to be charged. Those that do not will be returned to the traveler.

APPENDIX

BUSINESS MEAL ALLOWABLE RATES

Locations:	Breakfast	Lunch	Dinner
Fredericksburg	$6	$9	$20
Richmond	$7	$10	$24
Washington D. C.	$8	$12	$28
Other-In-State	$6	$9	$20

For out-of-state meals, use the Table of Meal Rates travelers utilize for overnight travel.

MILEAGE REIMBURSEMENT RATES
$.27/mile when use of a personally-owned vehicle is beneficial to the College such as when the car must be left at an airport for an extended period or if the round trip mileage is less than 100 miles or a State vehicle is unavailable.

$.19/mile when a personally-owned vehicle is used for the convenience of the College faculty or staff member.

Travel Request Form
Murray Library, Messiah College

_____

Name _____ Date _____

Event _____

Sponsoring Organization _____

Place _____

Inclusive dates of travel _____

Purpose *(Attach program description if available.)*:
❑ Job Training   ❑ Professional Development

Estimated Costs	
Registration	_____
Transportation	_____
Lodging	_____
Meals	_____
Misc.	_____
TOTAL	_____

❑ Check this box if you would like to reserve a college car and list below your departure and return times.

Date and time of car pick-up:

_____

Date and time of car return:

_____

❑ Check this box if you would like your registration processed and attach the <u>completed</u> form.

Traveler's Signature _____

Claim for Reimbursement forms – with receipts attached – should be signed by the Library Director. Forward the white copy to the Business Office; give the yellow copy to the Director's Assistant; keep the pink copy for your file.

Cash Advance forms should be completed by the traveler and submitted to the Business Office.

❑ Approval of immediate supervisor _____ Date _____
❑ Approval of Director _____ Date _____

USE OF COLLEGE RESOURCES

Travel on College Business

College employees must purchase all airline and rail tickets through C____/W_____ Travel in Middlebury, with whom the college has a contract. The College will not reimburse individuals or pay other travel agents for airline or rail tickets unless there is a written confirmation from C____/W_____ that they cannot match a quote from another agency for the same itinerary or written approval by the comptroller and assistant treasurer of Middlebury College.

C____/W_____ bills airline and rail tickets to the College when it has the employee's ID number and a budget number.

Travelers who charge domestic flights to the College through C____/W_____ receive $200,000 of life insurance.

Middlebury College has direct billing arrangements with several vendors at Burlington Airport to provide parking for College personnel traveling on College business. Faculty and staff may park at these facilities by displaying their College ID cards and filling out the paperwork required by each vendor. It is important when using this option to note clearly on the forms provided by the respective vendors your name, college ID number, and the department code to which the expense is to be assigned. The vendors are P___ and S_____, located at the north end of the Burlington terminal in a separate lot; B_____ A___ R____, located inside the terminal with drop-off at the return rental lot; and T_____ A___ R____, located on the north side of Williston Road just west of the intersection with Airport Drive.

Consult C____/W_____ prior to making hotel reservations.

The College anticipates that employees traveling by rail or air on College business will travel to departure points by personal vehicle. The College reimburses the expenses of such vehicle use. The use of taxis or limousines to travel from Middelbury to rail or air departures will be reimbursed at only standard mileage and daily parking rates as though personal vehicles had been used.

Any exception to this policy must have the prior written approval of the department head and the comptroller. Requests for exceptions should document extenuating circumstances or proposed overall savings to the College

Employees traveling on College business are expected to exercise the same care in incurring expense as a prudent person traveling for personal reasons.

Original receipts must accompany all vouchers submitted for travel expenses.

The College distinguishes between personal entertainment in most cases is not reimbursable. Personal entertainment is defined as, but not limited to, sporting-event tickets, theater tickets, movies in a hotel room, cost of alcoholic beverages, etc.

Address questions regarding travel policy to the budget manager in the Comptroller's Office.

Middlebury College has an American Express corporate card account to minimize the number of cash advances. The card bears both the employee's name and the name of the College and is to be used only for College business. All charges made on the card are billed directly to the employee at home. The annual charge for the card is billed directly to the College.

Employees are responsible for paying their American Express corporate card bills. Charges made while on College business will be reimbursed when a detailed formal accounting of expenses is presented to the Comptroller's Office. Requests for corporate credit cards are submitted to the Assistant Treasurer's Office by the employee's supervisor.

The College makes travel advances available for individuals who do not have a College credit card. Requests for travel advances must be submitted on the proper voucher form indicating the travel dates, business purposes, and the amount of advance requested. The voucher must be approved by the department head. Travel-advance checks are available in the Cashier's Office on Friday mornings for requests received in the Comptroller's Office by 5 P.M. the previous Tuesday.

Formal accounting for travel advances must be submitted to the Comptroller's Office immediately upon return from a trip. This accounting must include original receipts for meals, hotel accommodations, transportation, etc., and must be approved by the department head.

Internal Revenue Service regulations require that we substantiate all expenditures for travel and entertainment by adequate records. This substantiation must include information relating to: (1) the amount of the expenditure, (2) the time and place of the expenditure, (3) the business purpose of the expenditure, and (4) the names and the business relationships of individuals other than yourself for whom the expenditures are made. Vouchers lacking this information cannot be processed and must be returned to the originator

Reasonable incidental expenditures of $10 or less do not require documentation

For travel expenses other than airfare/train fares, employees may choose one of two reimbursement methods:

1. Per diem: Per diem rates are set by the U. S. government, and are intended to cover both accommodations and meals/incidental expenses. No receipts are needed for per diem reimbursement, but one receives only the amount set for the city/region which one has visited. Under this method, one need only submit a voucher to the budget administrator requesting per
diem reimbursement, specifying the city. (Conference registration fees must always be documented for reimbursement, however.)

2. Receipted reimbursement: To be reimbursed for all expenditures, employees must present original receipts with a prepared voucher to the budget administrator. No expense will be reimbursed without a receipt. Since per diem rates rarely suffice to cover the expense of lodging, meals, and incidentals, this method will usually be to the employee's advantage.

Travel advances in excess of the expenses submitted must be returned to the College upon completion of the travel. If such excess amounts are not returned within a reasonable time, they will be treated as taxable income, subject to the appropriate withholding tax.

No subsequent advance will be made available if the accounting for a previous travel advance is more than 30 days overdue.

If you seek reimbursement for travel expenditures paid from your own resources, you will need to provide documentation as detailed above.

USE OF PERSONAL CARS/MILEAGE REIMBURSEMENT

The College reimburses employees who use their own vehicles on trips for official College business on a per-mile driven basis. It reviews the reimbursement rate annually.

All requests for reimbursement must be submitted to the Comptroller's Office on an official expense voucher form and must be approved by the department head. The submitted forms must include details of the dates, points of departure and arrival, and miles driven.

Reimbursement is by check and includes properly documented tolls and parking costs. Parking or traffic violation fines and other tickets are the responsibility of the employee.

STAFF DEVELOPMENT COMMITTEE

The Staff Development Committee assists in the identification of and distribution of funds for voluntarily-selected professional development and training activities pursued by the library staff. To this end, the SDC maintains a webpage of links to professional development opportunities and calendars. The committee manages funding for job-related activities that enhance the skills of the attendees and support the library's mission. In addition, the SDC works with other library committees to develop and fund in-house activities in which the whole library staff can participate.

Staff Development Travel Funding Information

The SDC determines reimbursement by applying a <u>formula</u> approved by Library Forum to the expenses reported by the library staff. Rather than assigning a certain amount of money that each staff member may spend each year, we try to guarantee the full funding, according to the formula, of one trip per staff member each year. This means that some people may get several hundred dollars reimbursement, having spent a lot of money to go to a conference in California, while others may get fifty dollars reimbursed for a one-day workshop in Cleveland. It also means that at full funding, some people will have 100% of their expenses reimbursed while others will have significant out-of-pocket expenses. Each staff member may choose, in consultation with his/her supervisor, the staff development opportunities that most interest her or him, and we hope that the balance among modest trips, expensive trips, and no trips each year is within our financial ability to fund (this year's budget is $12,500). The guidelines are the following:

Per Diem

$65/day up to four nights away -- for each night spent away from home, you will be reimbursed $65 up to a maximum of $260. Travel days that do not involve a night away from home are reimbursed at a rate of $30. This per diem is intended to cover lodging and meals. If one's per diem expenses are less than the reimbursement the excess may be used to cover unreimbursed expenses in the transportation and registration categories, as long as the total reimbursement does not exceed the total expenditure.

Examples:

- departs on 10/1, returns on 10/5: 4 nights/5 days = $260
- departs on 10/1, returns on 10/2: 1 night/2 days = $95
- departs on 10/1, returns on 10/10: 9 nights/10 days = $260

Transportation

Full reimbursement of the first $200 of transportation expenses, plus 1/2 of the next $300 for a total possible reimbursement of $350. Transportation expenses include airfare, trainfare, busfare, gas or mileage (currently $.31/ mile) parking, cabfare, etc.

Examples:

- Transportation total cost $198 = $198
- Transportation total cost $300 = $250
- Transportation total cost $600 = $350

Registration

Full reimbursement of registration or tuition costs up to $200 plus 1/2 of the remainder (within reason). In the past, we have covered the registration costs of two events attended as part of the same trip, such as an ALA pre-conference plus the regular conference registration.

Examples:

- Conference registration $89 = $89
- Conference registration $200 = $200
- Tuition $500= $350
- Tuition $5,000 =forget it!!!!

Funding Application procedures

If you need an advance, you must submit an <u>APPLICATION FOR STAFF DEVELOPMENT FUNDS</u> to the SDC bookkeeper, currently <u>Megan Mitchell</u>. Please give as much detail as you can about the expenses you can predict, and supply a specific amount you wish to be advanced. The Controller's Office cuts checks twice a week, so please submit requests for advances as soon as you know your needs, and no later than 3 weeks before your departure date, to ensure the delivery of your advance check in time. Upon your return, you must submit an <u>EXPENSE REPORT FOR STAFF TRAVEL</u>, including original receipts for all expenditures. Any additional reimbursement will be processed at that time.

We ask that you submit expense reports for all staff development activities in which you participate, even if you don't expect funding. The committee reports each year the total out-of-pocket expenses of the library staff for staff development, and it is occasionally within our means to provide additional support for these trips.

Travel required as a representative of the library (OhioLINK meetings, for example) or required or encouraged by the library (NOTSL meetings, for example) is reimbursed out of the staff travel fund administered by <u>Alan Boyd</u>. Use the same <u>EXPENSE REPORT FOR STAFF TRAVEL</u>, accompanied by the originals of your receipts to apply for funding.

The library provides funding and release time for individual professional development activities with the expectation that the attendees will share knowledge, documents, and contacts from their experiences. No one method of reporting is appropriate to all types of events and the participant's judgement is essential to the process. The library requires, at a minimum:

- An <u>announcement</u> in staff news, either before or immediately after the event, providing the name or type of event attended. This allows interested staff to contact the attendee for individual consultations
- Active contact with staff members who will benefit from specifics from the conference

In addition, employees should seriously consider written reports, presentations at departmental or library-wide meetings, and/or ad hoc topic-specific meetings.

INFORMAL LIBRARY TRAVEL POLICY

All library staff, including part-time employees, are eligible to request reimbursement for professionally related travel expenses. If available funds cannot cover all requested travel, professional librarians receive first priority. Although, in theory, any staff member can apply for funding for air travel and room and board, in practice non-professional staff are generally limited to local, one-day events. Professional librarians can attend multi-day national conferences or workshops. A librarian presenting a paper may have his/her travel funded by the Vice-President for Academic Administration from a non-library budget line. Full funding for all expenses is usually provided; however, if insufficient funds are available a staff member may opt to pay part of the cost of a trip personally rather than forego the opportunity altogether. The College also provides each individual faculty member (including professional librarians) a $250 annual professional development fund. This money may be used for authorized travel.

At the start of each year, all library staff are asked to project their travel expenditures for the year in order to allow the Director, who makes the final decisions, to allocate funds as equitably as possible. However, inevitable changes throughout the year make accurate planning virtually impossible, so the policy ends up being more one of "first come, first served".

SIGNIFICANT PROFESSIONAL ACTIVITY - LIBRARY FACULTY

The Faculty Manual states the importance of scholarly and creative activity as a grounding for teaching. It also states that "the college gives primary emphasis to effective undergraduate teaching." Paraphrasing this, the librarians value scholarly and creative activity, but give primary emphasis to filling the responsibilities of their positions on the College library faculty. The demands of these positions differ from those placed on most position to position. Additional significant professional activity can be expected to reflect this diversity.

Formal teaching may require physical presence in the classroom for six to nine hours a week, and perhaps as many hours devoted to advising, help sessions, and labs. The remainder of a teachers duties may be scheduled more flexibly. In contrast, the librarians' work schedule has usually been a forty hour week in the library, since their work is closely involved with the staff, the collections, and users. It is difficult to spend much of the time on other significant professional activity. Moreover, librarians, like department chairs, have certain administrative functions, and scheduling allowances are made in recognition of this. They have ten or (for the College Librarian, Systems Librarian and Archivist) eleven month schedules which allow a catch-up period in the summer.

In the absence of more flexible scheduling and large blocks of time conductive to research (except during sabbaticals), the librarians believe that their additional professional activities should usually be given less weight than is the case with classroom teachers. They should be pursued only to the extent that they do not interfere with primary responsibilities.

Librarians differ from other faculty in more than their work schedule. The field of library/archival science is not exactly comparable to disciplines such as history or physics. The terminal degree is the master's, following an undergraduate degree with a major in some "subject" area. Academic librarians usually couple their training and expertise in library/archival science with a strong interest and academic background in another discipline. Therefore, it may be as appropriate for librarians to pursue graduate study in one of these disciplines, to do creative work in them, and to participate in their professional associations, as to carry out these activities in library/archival science.

The St. Olaf librarians have agreed upon the following list of additional significant professional activities, which should be given more weight when considering promotion to associate and full professor. The two areas of activity listed under category I are of equal importance. Although the categories are listed in descending order of importance, they are relative and there may be some overlap.

I. **PUBLICATIONS, UNPUBLISHED WORKS, ORAL PRESENTATIONS AND CREATIVE WORK OR PERFORMANCE** such as: that relating directly to library science or disciplines related to the librarian's duties. Evaluation will be based on the jurying provided by the publisher or, in the case of unpublished works, internal or external evaluators.

    ACTIVITY IN PROFESSIONAL ORGANIZATIONS BEYOND THAT NORMALLY EXPECTED OF MEMBERS, such as: leadership roles which contribute significantly to policy decisions or programs, at the national, regional and state level. Evaluation will be based on the scope and scale of work involved, as demonstrated to internal or external evaluators.

SIGNIFICANT PROFESSIONAL ACTIVITY – LIBRARY FACULTY (cont.)

II. **ADDITIONAL STUDY OR TRAINING** beyond the normal in-service workshops or seminars required by the librarian's position, as for a supplemental advanced degree in library science or in another academic discipline.

III. **HONORS, AWARDS AND GRANTS**
   1. From external sources.
   2. Refereed by St. Olaf or another employer.

RATIONALE

The two categories comprising level one in this statement provide substantial. different. benefits. Publications, oral presentations, and other types of creative endeavor may enhance the reputation of the . faculty member, the department, and the College. Ideally this activity will also improve job performance by renewing interests and broadening knowledge. The amount of research or other effort required by an oral presentation or creative work may equal to that demanded by many kinds of publication. so that they should be accorded the same relative weight.

Involvement in professional organizations in a capacity which influences the experience or performance of others possesses many of the same benefits as publication. It has the advantage (which it shares with oral presentations and other types of personal contact) of providing for the immediate exchange of ideas. Among librarians it has additional importance because of the pressing needs of systems networking, national and international standards, and the speed with which technological changes take place. Professional organizations fill a major role in setting priorities and standards. as well as disseminating information.

Section II. reflects the fact that the master's degree in library science is the terminal degree in the field. (In the case of the Archivist. the terminal degree may be either a master's degree in history. augmented by courses in archival methods. or a master's degree in library science with a concentration in archives.) Further graduate study, or some sort of technical training, may be valuable to librarians. depending upon the individual situation. This study may be in library and information science. or it may be in some academic discipline. development. reference, etc.

Job skills workshops and career development programs can be important aspects of continuing education, and are supported by the Library. Library employees are expected to attend job skills workshops and are encouraged to seek career development programs. Participation in College committee meetings, other Library-related committee meetings, and library association meetings is also encouraged.

Job Skills Workshops

Department Coordinators are expected to make staff aware of appropriate training, and staff should attend MINITEX, OCLC, III, and other workshops when they are offered. Registration fees. mileage. parking, and necessary meal expenses will be paid by the Library as budget permits.

Career Development Workshops

Attendance at career development workshops is not required but is encouraged. In general Library employees are entitled to attend career development workshops when it is determined by the individual and the Department Coordinator to meet the goal of development of career related skills. All individuals attending career development workshops are encouraged to share pertinent information with other staff members at the next staff meeting, or in a brief memo. It may not be possible for the Library to fund more than one career development workshop per person in any given year.

Meetings

Library employees are encouraged to become members of College committees. and are able to attend such meetings when they do not interfere unduly with the work of the department of the Library. Library staff who are members of ongoing off-campus committees should make arrangements with their Department Coordinator regarding the time involved. In some cases. membership on a long-term campus or non-campus committee may be considered a temporary adjustment in the individual's job description. The "Request" form is not required for ongoing committee assignments. Library employees who are members of Library organizations, such as the Minnesota Library Association. may require time to attend meetings.

Procedures For Application

The "Workshop/Meeting/Conference Request" form should be filled out as completely as possible. at least one week in advance of the event. Approval must be given by the Department Coordinator. The College Librarian may have to approve the request if funding needs to be provided. Approval may not be granted if attendance would interfere with the smooth functioning of the department or Library or if the request seems unreasonable in its purpose. Funding may not be possible for all events. even if time is granted.

1/18/89, 11/9/93 Language update to reflect position title changes, 2/96

Setting aside some time each month by Library faculty for the pursuit of projects leading to publication and professional enrichment (such as auditing courses at St. Olaf or another college, doing research for an article or book, or the actual writing of an article or book) is desirable. Attendance at professional workshops and conferences, serving on committees, consulting and lecturing outside the college, as well as keeping up with the profession by reading professional journals are all covered explicitly or implicitly in the Faculty Manual. Although there may be some difficulty in implementing a policy that can be applied equitable to full-time and part-time library faculty, we make the following recommendations:

- That eight hours each month for full-time faculty, pro-rated for anyone working part-time, be allowed each individual to pursue research or professional development, up to 80 hours per academic year. The brevity of time in December when classes are in session should not present any problem since the break after exams can be used to augment time set aside during the first part of the month.

- These hours may be accumulated during the month from hours set aside each week. In most circumstances these will be used up during the month, but in certain cases (determined by limitations in the individual's schedule or the need for in-depth research away from campus) these may be accumulated beyond the month but must be used before the end of the academic year.

- Professional development time should be used at times when the presence of the individual is not required in the Library or when the absence of the individual does not make an unjust impact on the schedule of her/his colleagues. Prior notification of intent to take advantage of this time should be made to any colleagues affected, just as it is made in the case of attending professional meetings or consulting and lecturing outside the college.

Approved by the Library Faculty - 12/93

1.10   FACULTY DEVELOPMENT

1.10.1   Application Procedure

The application for funds should be sent to the current chair of the Faculty Welfare and Development Committee and should meet the following requirements:

A.   Ten copies of a one-page summary should be submitted. Attached to the first copy (or original) of your request, include a complete description of the program or project for which the application for funding is being made.

    If possible, include a copy of brochures, programs, etc.

B.   The summary page should include the following items:

    1.   Dates of the program or project.
    2.   A budget, including the following:
        a.   The total estimated costs of the project,
        b.   Any funding from other sources, such as departmental funding,
        c.   Exact amount of funding requested from the Faculty Welfare and Development Committee (estimates are discouraged since they may result in unused faculty development funds that could be awarded to deserving development projects), and
        d.   Funding carried by the individual.
    3.   A brief paragraph stating why this project merits funding. Please include special considerations, conference responsibilities/involvements, and the unique benefits of the request to your professional development.

1.10.2   Award Criteria

The criteria for the decision to recommend an award:

A.   The Provost informs the committee of the amount available for funds for the academic year.

B.   The decision process/criteria:
    1.   The committee screens requests according to:
        a.   Applications for funds needed during the current fiscal year (before June 30),
        b.   Applications that are appropriate in purpose (e.g. Develop the faculty member directly), and
        c.   Provide all the information that the application procedure requests.

    2.   The committee may also screen according to the:
        a.   Amount of personal and/or departmental commitment to the project,
        b.   Amount of awards applicant has received in the past two to three years,
        c.   Merit of proposal, and
        d.   Clarity and depth of information on application.

C.   The committee's recommendations are sent to the provost for final approval/selection.

<u>Policy for Use of Library's Travel/Staff Development Budget</u>

Staff development for library staff at all levels receives a high priority in duPont Library. Staffing costs constitute the largest category of expenditures in the library budget each year. Therefore, use of travel/staff development funds is open to all permanent full- or part- time library staff members, since personal and professional development are expected of all staff members.

DuPont Library has adopted the following three levels of travel priority:

a) Travel which contributes to the effectiveness of the whole library, that is, which contributes directly to the library's mission and goals.

b) Travel which contributes primarily to the effectiveness of the staff member's department and its specific mission and goals.

c) Travel which contributes primarily to an individual staff member's personal and professional goals and growth.

The travel policy consists of the following provisos:

1. Individual staff members will discuss their training and staff development needs with their supervisors on a regular basis. Likewise, supervisors may recommend or require that a staff member pursue training in a specific area. All requests to the University Librarian for approval to draw on training/staff development funds must have the supervisor's formal approval.

2. The attached form must be completed and submitted to the University Librarian for his approval.

3. Staff who have used library funds to travel for staff development have a responsibility to find a way to share with other appropriate staff members what they have learned.

4. If more than one staff member is attending a given meeting, workshop, or conference, staff are expected to share a room unless this arrangement results in the sharing of rooms by members of the opposite sex.

5. Because ALA is the principle professional organization for all library staff, it is important for all staff members to have an opportunity to attend the ALA annual meeting from time to time, on a rotating basis, with due attention given to maintaining an appropriate balance between exempt and

non-exempt staff. The library will cover the travel expenses and registration of up to 4 staff members each year.

6. Travel which a staff member is requested or required to do by his/her supervisor, or travel which is required of a staff member by virtue of his/her position or job description will be fully funded from the library budget.

7. Travel to receive training to maintain or enhance a staff member's level of competence or job related skills will be fully funded from the library budget.

8. Partial or full funding may be available to enable staff to engage in professional activities.

A major goal in administering the use of travel/staff development funds in duPont Library is to put as few constraints as possible on fund usage.

In the event that the library experiences a significant reduction in staff development funding in the budget, this policy will be reviewed and modified as necessary.

It is the responsibility of the University Librarian to monitor use of staff development funds and to ensure equity of access among the entire staff.

08/31/00

TRAVEL GUIDELINES

The Library is committed to supporting travel and registration for conferences and training sessions for the entire staff from the allocation in the regular Library budget. The following guidelines apply:

1. All travel requests must be approved by the immediate supervisor who will determine whether the particular request is job related, essential or required.

2. All professional staff have a $50.00 deductible to be applied toward travel requests per academic year. This deductible will be waived for support staff.

3. All travel which is required for the job will be reimbursed at 100% minus the deductible. All other travel will be reimbursed at 75%.

4. For staff presenting papers at a conference, the Library will reimburse for one Library-related conference per year at 75% of the total cost.

5. Any exceptions will be determined by the Library Director.

Note: Library faculty should apply for Career Development Funds as appropriate.

WILLIAM PATERSON UNIVERSITY

TRAVEL

For a Specific Inquiry, click on any of the following

NEW!
Employee Travel Request and Expense Voucher Forms

- Regulation
- Approval
- Reimbursable Expenses
- Non-Reimbursable Expenses
- Conferences, Meetings and Training Sessions
- Transportation
- Prospective Employees
- Air Tickets
- Staff Reimbursement
- Travel Advancement
- Required Receipts
- Guest Meals
- Exceptions

Regulation

These travel regulations apply to our University staff, prospective employees, and others authorized to travel on behalf of William Paterson University. Compliance with these procedures is the responsibility of the individual traveling on official University business. The regulations apply to all official University travel regardless of the source of funds. All University reimbursement requests must be filed during the fiscal year the expense was incurred. Reimbursement requests for prior years will not be payable from the current fiscal year.

Approval

Approval is required from the appropriate Dean, Director, Vice President, or designee for all individuals prior to traveling on official University business. Travel related to student teaching, off-campus nursing program, and special day trip assignments (mileage only) do not require the submission of a travel authorization. A completed registration form and literature listing conference dates, hotel accommodations, inclusive meals and ground transportation provided by the hosting organization, if applicable, should be attached to the Employee Travel Approval form. After approval by the appropriate authorities, the request will be forwarded to the Office of Business Services to ensure compliance with University travel policies.

Reimbursable Expenses

Travel expenses are restricted to those costs that are required to transact official University business. An individual traveling on authorized University business is expected to exercise the same care in incurring expenses that a prudent person would exercise if traveling on personal business at his/her own expense. Specific reimbursable expenses are included in the University's travel policies.

Non-Reimbursable Expenses

Some expenses cannot be reimbursed. They include:

Alcoholic beverages;

Spouse or family members' travel costs;

Telephone calls that are non-business related;

Lost/stolen cash or personal property;

In-Room Movies;

Meals for one-day trips not including overnight lodging;

Normal noonday lunch;

Trip/Flight insurance;

Personal items and services, e.g., toiletries, luggage, clothes, haircuts, shoeshine, etc.;

Laundry, cleaning and pressing costs;

Avoidable expenses for non-business related activities, such as sightseeing tours, etc.;

Meals included in the cost of airfare or registration fees;

Repairs, towing service, lubrication, car washes, etc., for personal vehicles;

Taxi or related transportation expenses to/from hotel to restaurants (unless unusual circumstances prevail).

Child care costs;

Conferences, Meetings and Training Sessions

Staff members requesting permission to attend conferences, meetings and training sessions must request advance approval through the completion of a Travel Authorization Form. It is University policy that all travel that will be in excess of 24-hour periods requiring overnight lodging has an allowable per diem reimbursement.

• Lodging

Lodging accommodations are restricted to standard/first-class hotels/motels. When lodging is shared with others, reimbursement is limited to the individual's share of the cost. Original itemized receipts are required. Managers should use the government per diem rates as a guide when approving lodging costs. Expenses in excess of the maximum may be reimbursed if accompanied by a written explanation and subject to approval of the Vice President for Administration and Finance or designee.

• Meals

Actual expenses for meals, taxes and tips are reimbursable up to the maximum allowed by government per diem rates (less $2.00) at the following website: "www. Policyworks.gov/main/mt/homepage/mtt/perdiem/travel.shtml". For reimbursement in excess of these maximum allowable rates, original detailed hotel/motel receipts accompanied by a written explanation and subject to approval of the Vice President for Administration and Finance or designee is required. Alcoholic beverages are not allowed for reimbursement on Federal, Sponsored or State Funded accounts.

• Registration Fees

Registration fees for conventions, conferences, workshops, meetings, and like activities are reimbursable if not paid in advance. Original receipts must be submitted to receive reimbursement. The University will pay in advance registration fees in excess of $50. On the travel approval form there is a box which indicates whether the University or the employee is paying the registration fee, if prepayment is required, please attach a completed Voucher Payment Form along with appropriate registration materials to the back of the Employee Travel Request and Approval form.

• Telephone

Telephone charges incurred while traveling will be reimbursed when such costs relate directly to University business. For overnight travel, personal calls in excess of one call to an individual's home per day will not be reimbursed unless a written explanation is provided and approved by the Vice President for Administration and Finance or designee.

Transportation

• Public

○ (a) Air, Rail, Bus: The most economical class of travel will be used. First-class travel is not permitted. The Original passenger receipts are required for air, rail, and bus travel.

- (b) **Taxicabs and Limousine Service:** Necessary taxicab charges including reasonable gratuities are permitted but only in emergencies or if public transportation is not readily available. Travel to and from airports and downtown areas should be confined to regular, scheduled limousine service whenever such service is less costly than taxi. Expenses in excess of $5 require a receipt. Reimbursement will be allowed if the traveler chooses to take a taxi or limo when courtesy (no charge) transportation is offered from/to the airport/hotel.

- **Private Vehicles**

  - (a) When a privately owned vehicle is used for University business travel, the individual operating the privately owned vehicle must carry motor vehicle liability insurance and so certify on the Travel Expense Voucher Form. Expenses for repair of privately owned vehicles being used for business are the travelers' responsibility.
  - (b) Individuals using privately owned vehicles for authorized University business will be reimbursed for mileage at the rate authorized by the State of New Jersey and for tolls and parking. Currently, the State of New Jersey mileage reimbursement rate is 25 cents per mile.

- **University-Owned Motor Vehicles**

  University-owned vehicles may be used by University staff on official University business subject to availability.

  - (a) Operators are required to have a valid driver's license.
  - (b) Request vehicles through the Director of Facilities via a request memorandum from the appropriate Dean, Director, or Vice President indicating reason, destination, approximate miles, date(s) and other individuals traveling in the vehicles.
  - (c) The University vehicle credit card is to be used for gas and oil. The University vehicle credit card will be provided by the Business Services. The card and all receipts must be returned the first workday following the University-owned vehicle use. The Business Services will maintain a log of credit card use. The log will include: card issuer, card number, authorized user, date of card issuance, date of card return, total of receipts returned with card, and account number to be charged. This log will be used in reconciliation of credit card statements. Credit cards will be secured when not in use. Department budgets will be charged for credit card expenses.
  - (d) Expenses for tolls and parking will be reimbursed at the actual cost incurred.
  - (e) Operators are responsible for penalties due to motor vehicle infractions.

- **Motor Vehicle Rentals**

  Motor vehicle rentals may be permitted under extenuating circumstances where commercial transportation facilities are not available or their use is impractical. Travelers should be prepared to cost justify the use of rental cards and should describe extenuating circumstances on the Employee Travel Approval form. A compact car must be rented unless three or more staff members will be traveling in the rented vehicle. Gasoline, tolls, parking, etc., expenses are reimbursable. Original itemized receipts must be submitted for reimbursement. When renting an automobile, with approval, employees should use their Corporate American Express Cards. American Express covers the employee for the Collision/Loss Damage Waiver.

Prospective Employees

Only prospective employees who are invited for University position interviews are eligible for reimbursement of travel expenses. Approval to invite a prospective professional employee is only authorized by the Dean/Director or the Provost Office. Prospective employees who wish reimbursement of travel expenses must complete and submit a voucher with original receipts to substantiate the expenditures to the chairperson of the interviewing committee. Reimbursement will be at the same rates as paid to the University staff. The voucher form must then be approved by the appropriate Dean/Director/Provost designee by signing in appropriate certification area of the form and submitted to the Controllers Office for entrance into the University financial system and issuance of a check.

Air Tickets

The University can purchase airline tickets for staff members traveling on University business through the official travel agency of the University, Stratton Travel Management. Stratton Travel can be reached at (888) 390-8728 and our agents name is Sharon Rubinson. It is important to remember that to get the best choice of seating and accommodations, all travel forms and arrangements must be completed as early as possible. Delays in processing these forms in any office could result in higher ticket prices. Please note, Stratton Travel will not issue any business related airline/train tickets until given the authority to do so by the Travel Desk. If the staff member purchases the airline ticket, reimbursement will be made after travel has taken place.

Staff Reimbursement

Staff members, prospective employees, and others traveling on official University business are reimbursed through the completion and submissions of a Travel Expense Voucher Form to Business Services. The voucher shall show dates, point of departure, and destination for each trip and be prepared by typewriter or printed clearly in ink. All original receipts must be attached. Reimbursement will not be made prior to the completion of travel. Reimbursements will be processed through the Accounts Payable unit of Business Services. Travel Expense Vouchers will be reviewed for completeness, compliance with allowable expenses and limits, required receipts, and authorizing signatures. Approved vouchers will then be entered into the FRS system for "demand" issuance of a reimbursement check.

Travel Advance

Unless there are extenuating circumstances, the University will not provide travel advances. This includes the prepayment of hotel expenses. Employees who frequently travel should contact Mr. Walter Johnson (X-2242) for information concerning the WPUNJ Corporate American Express Card.

Required Receipts

(a) Air, rail, and bus;

(b) Hotel/motel;

(c) Conference fee;

(d) Expenditures above the maximum allowable rate;

(e) Receipts generally not required if less than $5.

Guest Meals

University business may require taking a guest for breakfast/lunch/dinner. Approval in advance must be obtained from the respective Vice President or designee.

Exceptions

Any exceptions to the University travel procedures require approval of the Vice President for Administration and Finance.

Leave of Absence Policies

Swarthmore College
Swarthmore, Pennsylvania

West Virginia Wesleyan College
Buckhannon, West Virginia

LEAVES

It is the policy of the College to grant periodic leaves of absence to continuing members of the faculty whose appointments are in the ranks of Professor, Associate Professor, Assistant Professor or Instructor. A leave with compensation from the College is conditioned on the presentation of a definite program of research, writings, or other activity that gives promise of increasing the future usefulness of the recipient to the College. Insofar as the resources of the College permit, such leaves may be granted as often as once in four years and are normally granted for a half-year at full salary or for a full year with as much as half-salary. (Members of the faculty whose temporary appointments extend into a fifth year or beyond are eligible, with the support of their departments, to submit a proposal for leave. It should be noted, however, that in such cases the criterion of the future usefulness to the College requires particularly careful evaluation.) With the approval of the Department Chair and the Provost, a faculty member may delay the leave by one year and be eligible for the next leave following two years of teaching. If a faculty member is the recipient of an outside grant or is paid for work during a leave, the payment from the College is reduced accordingly. A faculty member who receives full outside support for a year may, with the permission of the Department Chair and Provost, be granted an additional semester of leave with College funding, for a total of three continuous semesters.

For persons on probationary appointments, the period of probation will include time spent on leave of absence, subject to arrangements with the College concerning the purpose and duration of the leave.

Full-time or part-time leaves of absence without compensation may be granted subject to particular arrangements between the faculty member and the College. Such absence will not be counted as leave time or as part of the probationary period.

In addition to these matters, established in a joint Board-Faculty policy statement, the College expects faculty members who receive leaves paid for wholly or in part by Swarthmore College to return to their teaching responsibilities at the College for at least one year after the year of leave. The College expects faculty members who do not return to repay the College for the amount of their leave support. (This section is based on College regulations and practices dating from the 1950s. See also CEP recommendations 123, adopted, as amended, by the faculty, 24 May 1968.)

XI. Faculty Development

The Wesleyan faculty member is expected to seek opportunities to continue professional growth. He or she is encouraged to attend summer institutes, participate in faculty seminars, attend professional meetings and be generally alive to the recent developments in his or her discipline and higher education in general. The College will encourage and seek to support plans for faculty development.

A. The College Leave and Assistance Program

At West Virginia Wesleyan College the Leave and Assistance Program is an integral part of the overall plan for faculty development and evaluation. Such a program is one of the most important means by which a faculty member's teaching effectiveness may be enhanced, his or her scholarly usefulness enlarged, and the College's academic program strengthened and developed. The program provides opportunity for continued professional growth and new or renewed intellectual achievement through study, research, writing and travel.

General considerations:

1. This Leave and Assistance Program is not regarded as deferred compensation to which a faculty member is entitled automatically, as in the case of certain fringe benefits.
2. Flexibility is desirable in the administration of this program. Needs, interests and assignments of faculty change; the needs of the College may change as the clientele change or as new programs are instituted.
3. Available resources will be administered in such a manner as to balance opportunities for professional development among and within different academic fields.

B. Types of Support Available

Ordinarily, support for faculty development will take one of four forms: sabbatical leave, leave without assistance, developmental assistance, and support for participation in professional societies and workshops.

1. Sabbatical Leave

   A sabbatical leave is a leave of absence which is designed to enhance the professional growth of a faculty member. A sabbatical may be used, for example: to gather material for a book or publication, to write these; to provide time for creative endeavors--painting, sculpture, etc.; to pursue disciplined studies.

   a. Eligibility

      i. After six contract years a faculty member is eligible to apply for a year's leave at two-thirds of his or her basic salary or one semester's leave at full salary.
      ii. After three contract years a faculty member is eligible to apply for a semester's leave at two-thirds of his or her basic salary.
      iii. Eligibility for the next sabbatical begins with the academic year following the sabbatical that was granted.

      For faculty on sabbatical leave at two-thirds salary, all fringe benefits shall continue.

b. Application Procedure

The normal deadline for receiving proposals for sabbatical leaves by the Dean of the College is November 15 preceding the academic year during which the leave is requested.

2. Leaves Without Compensation

A faculty member may request a leave of absence without compensation to pursue personal professional objectives.

The normal deadline for receiving proposals for leaves without compensation by the Dean of the College is November 15 preceding the academic year during which the leave is requested.

Normally, for faculty on leave without compensation, their Retirement Annuity Insurance and Collective Life Insurance benefits are discontinued for the leave period. A faculty member may elect to keep his or her hospitalization and major medical benefits in force by paying both the College's portion and his or her portion of the monthly premiums for the duration of the leave period.

A faculty member on leave is not eligible for total disability insurance benefits or for tuition waiver.

3. Developmental Assistance

Developmental assistance may take the form of stipends for summer study or research, leaves, adjusted or reduced teaching loads, financial assistance for work toward a terminal degree, low interest loan, or a combination of these.

For proposals involving a semester or year's leave, reduced teaching load, or summer stipend, the normal deadline for receiving proposals by the Dean of the College is February 15 preceding the academic year during which the assistance is requested.

Fringe benefits cannot be guaranteed.

4. Procedures for Leaves or Assistance

a. Normally, a proposal is subject to the approval of the college administration with the advice of the Professional Affairs Committee. The proposal should take into consideration the faculty member's most recent evaluation and plan for professional development. The proposal, which shall be in writing, should include such advance plans as are likely to assure productive results.

A clear statement of plans is especially important in proposals for developmental assistance, for which remuneration is based on needs or expenses rather than a stated proportion of the faculty member's salary.

b. A report and evaluation of the activities undertaken within this program usually should be made to the faculty member's department and to the Dean of the College. The report also should be included in the faculty member's file of professional activities.

c. Recipients of leaves or major developmental assistance shall be obligated to return to the College for further service of one year subsequent to the leave. Each applicant for a sabbatical leave or a major development assistance program must sign an agreement to return to West Virginia Wesleyan College or to repay all monies received while on such a leave. Exceptions to this policy may be made by the President of the College in extenuating circumstances.

Leaves for medical or personal reasons are not covered in this program. (See Section XIV.)

5. Participation in Professional Societies and Workshops

    As part of their professional growth, faculty members are expected at their own expense to maintain memberships in scholarly societies, subscribe to journals, and participate in conferences and workshops.

    Assistance with the expenses of attendance at professional meetings and workshops will be provided, as funds are available and can be equitably apportioned in the following way:

    a. The College will pay 50% of the faculty member's expenses for attendance at meetings of learned societies, clinics, workshops, institutes or similar meetings of short duration when the faculty member attends on his or her own initiative for reasons of professional interest or advancement.
    b. The College will pay 100% of expenses if the faculty member has a place on the program, holds an office that necessitates his or her presence, or is requested by the College to attend as an official representative to a committee or association in which the College holds institutional membership.

    Requests for support (with careful estimate of expenses) must be made in advance through the Office of the Dean of the College. Reimbursement of expenses will be made upon submission of an account of actual expenses and detailed supporting evidence. Under extenuating circumstances an advance of funds may be available for all or a portion of the expected expense.

C. **Tuition Waiver for Faculty**

    Faculty are granted tuition waiver for graduate and undergraduate courses at **West Virginia Wesleyan College** when their enrollment does not create additional instructional salary expense.

    Faculty are eligible for limited waiver of tuition on graduate courses at **West Virginia University** in accordance with University policies. Only full-time Wesleyan employees are eligible. Requests for this privilege must be made about three months in advance through the Office of the Dean of the College at Wesleyan. Failure to give timely notice of intention not to use hours thus reserved may result in suspension of the privilege.

Sabbatical Policies

Albion College
Albion, Michigan

Alma College
Alma, Michigan

Arizona State University West
Phoenix, Arizona

Drew University
Madison, New Jersey

Gonzaga University
Spokane, Washington

Illinois Wesleyan University
Bloomington, Illinois

Linfield College
McMinnville, Oregon

Lipscomb University
Nashville, Tennessee

St. John's University/
College of St. Benedict
Collegeville, Minnesota

Sweet Briar College
Sweet Briar, Virginia

GUIDELINES FOR SABBATICAL APPLICATIONS
Revised 9/99

As you construct your sabbatical application, you may want to refer to the sabbatical policy in the *Faculty Handbook*. The Faculty Development Committee will evaluate applications on the basis of the quality of research, scholarship, creative activity, or other professional activity to be undertaken, using the following criteria, as set forth in the sabbatical policy:

> the importance of the project in its own right (for instance, in the context of the present state of scholarship in the particular area), the relationship of the project to improving the applicant's ability as a teacher, the relationship of the project to the applicant's longer term professional development plans, the relationship of the project to the goals and objectives of the college, other benefits to the individual and the college, the anticipated outcomes; and, for those who have had previous development support (such as sabbaticals or large grants), the benefits to the individual and college from that support.

(Note that all evaluation criteria are important, but that these various criteria can have different weight in different proposals.)

Your application must include all of the following:

1. the completed cover sheet

2. a description of the proposed project and anticipated benefits

3. If your sabbatical plans are contingent upon factors beyond your control, please provide the committee with an alternative project that you would undertake if your original plans do not materialize as you envision.

4. a letter of support from the department chair or, when the chair is the applicant, from the most senior (other) department faculty member

The proposal must be in the hands of the chair one week before the deadline for application in order that the chair have adequate time to prepare the support letter and staffing plan (see below).

5. a current curriculum vitae

Letters from institutions or from collaborators with whom you will work should be appended in those instances where collaborative studies will be undertaken.

Send copies of the complete application to all members of the Faculty Development Committee as well as two copies to the Office of Academic Affairs. The chair should send the support letter to all committee members and to the Office of Academic Affairs.

COVER SHEET FOR FACULTY DEVELOPMENT GRANT

Name of applicant(s)_____Date:_____

Position(s)_____

Grant Period: [ ] First semester   [ ] Second semester   [ ] Summer

Grant Type: [ ] Small grant   [ ] Large grant   [ ] Blanchard Fellowship

ABSTRACT OF GRANT PROPOSAL

BUDGET SUMMARY: (Receipts are required for the final report. A complete and detailed budget with full explanations may be attached.)

Budget	Amount(s) Requested	For each line requested, briefly explain the purpose

Other funds applied for to support this project:

Has this project or projects similar to it been supported for the applicant in the past? If yes, by whom?

If funds for travel or equipment are requested, please describe how departmental travel funds are being used. If you hold an endowed chair, please indicate the disposition of those funds.

(check list)   [ ] detailed and complete budget   [ ] letter(s) of support (where applicable)

Signature _____

Note: Send one copy of the completed proposal, including letters of support to the Office of Academic Affairs, one to each of the Committee members (   ), and one to   , Assistant to the Vice President for Academic Affairs.

VIII.   Provisions relating to tenured faculty.

A.   Sabbatical Leaves:

1.   Purpose

The primary purpose of a sabbatical leave program is to strengthen
Alma College by improving the quality of instruction and by
providing an opportunity for faculty members to engage in
meaningful professional pursuits for at least a short period of time,
during which they are freed from teaching and administrative
assignments. Individual proposals for sabbatical leave activity shall
be judged in the light of this purpose.

2.   Procedures

In September, the FPC in consultation with the Provost determines
those eligible for a sabbatical leave in the following year. The
Provost's Office shall send a written invitation to those eligible
faculty, requesting submission of a sabbatical application (see
Sabbatical Leave form). If any faculty member who considers
him/herself eligible has not received an invitation by the end of
September, he or she should inquire at the Provost's Office regarding
eligibility.

Applications shall be returned to the Provost's Office by the third
Monday in October preceding the academic year for which the leave
is requested. The applications shall be reviewed by FPC for
recommendation to the Provost; the final approval of sabbatical leaves
shall be made by the Provost who shall recommend such leaves to the
President, the Instruction and Faculty Committee of the Board of
Trustees and subsequently to the Board of Trustees. Approval shall
be announced following the winter Board meeting.

3.   Eligibility

Faculty members with tenure shall become eligible for sabbatical
leave in every seventh year of service at Alma College, except that no
sabbatical leave shall be granted during the year of probation which
may follow the 6-year Periodic Review of a tenured appointment (See

Section IX. E. 3.). Further, no sabbatical leave shall be granted which would begin less than one year prior to a faculty member's final year of teaching before retirement. In the event that an individual has at the request of the institution postponed applying for a sabbatical leave or implementing an approved leave, that individual's eligibility for a subsequent leave shall be calculated from the time that the prior sabbatical leave would have been (rather than from the time it actually was) taken.

Criteria and Restrictions

Each proposed sabbatical leave program shall be evaluated individually. Proposals should include the following information:

* a statement of the proposed leave: its intention, plan of activity and expected outcome(s);
* the relation of the plan to the person's teaching and/or scholarship and professional growth;

* the relations of the plan to the person's departmental objectives and curricula;

* the proposed implementation or application to the person's teaching and the benefit to Alma's students.

Factors to be considered in the evaluation of proposals shall include (1) the explanation/justification of the proposed activity, (2) the applicant's eligibility, (3) the number of sabbatical requests in a given academic year, (4) the needs of the department. If all requests for sabbatical leaves cannot be granted because of financial or staffing needs, priority shall normally be extended to requests for off-campus research and study programs, to seniority, and to the feasibility of release.

While professors are free to seek fellowships and grants to supplement their salary, they are not free to take a position for pay during the leave unless such use of the leave is approved by the Provost. Expected supplemental income shall be described and justified in the application for leave and any remunerated activities must be in conformity with and further the objectives of the specific sabbatical program.

For sabbatical leave programs, the College is under no obligation to provide facilities, equipment, travel expense and supplies. However, the faculty member on sabbatical may apply for Faculty Development Funds.

5.   Terms

The period of leave shall be for either Fall or Winter Term at full pay, or both Fall and Winter Terms at half pay; release from duties during Spring Term in connection with a sabbatical leave requires special arrangements with, and approval of, the Provost, in consultation with the Department Chair.

A sabbatical leave need not be taken in a single academic year but may be spaced out in full term segments over two consecutive years. Eligibility for sabbatical is to be reckoned from the beginning of the academic year in which the last preceding sabbatical was begun and includes only periods of full-time regular appointment (with the exceptions noted in 3. above).

Sabbatical leaves for librarians shall be for either 24 weeks (half-year) at full pay or 48 weeks (full-year) at one-half pay within a given contract year.

Faculty members on sabbatical leave do not serve on standing committees of the faculty or as academic advisors. A person on sabbatical leave is not expected to participate in College or Departmental matters but may do so as he or she chooses.

Fringe benefits shall be continued on the usual basis unless there are special circumstances.

6.   Obligation

A summary of the sabbatical leave shall be submitted to the Provost within three months following the completion of the leave; the summary shall be shared with the FPC and placed in the faculty member's professional file. This summary should include some reflection on the attainment of the goals of the leave and the application to one's teaching and professional growth.

Any professor accepting a sabbatical leave accepts an obligation to return to the College for one full year of service following the conclusion of the leave.

Provisions for all faculty.

A.   The College shall nurture a climate in which faculty shall be able to maximize their professional satisfaction and effectiveness. Current formal efforts, which should be reviewed annually for improvement, include the following:

1.   new faculty orientation and mentor program

Policy and Procedure

ASU ARIZONA STATE UNIVERSITY WEST		Number **ACDW 705**	
Manual Academic Affairs	Section Leaves and Absences	Page 1 of 6	
Subject Sabbatical Leave		Effective 2/28/1961	Revised 8/17/1997

PURPOSE   To describe policies and procedures for sabbatical leaves

SOURCES   *Arizona Board of Regents Policy Manual - 6-207*
President's Cabinet
Academic Senate
Office of the Vice President and Provost, ASU West

APPLICABILITY

Administrators with faculty rank and tenure who have completed six years of full-time service at ASU West

Faculty members who have achieved tenure and completed six years of full-time service with the rank of assistant professor or higher at ASU West

Academic professionals who have achieved continuing status and completed six years of full-time service at ASU West as probationary or continuing status academic professionals

POLICY

On the recommendation of the president, the Board of Regents may grant sabbatical leave to eligible administrators, faculty members, and academic professionals whose sabbatical applications have been approved at the academic unit level. A sabbatical leave is not deferred compensation to which an administrator, faculty member, or academic professional is entitled after six years of service.

Sabbaticals are the institution's investment in the future. Sabbaticals facilitate long-term vitality for faculty and academic professionals by enabling them to master state-of-the-art developments in their fields, to develop alternative approaches to research and teaching, and to acquire new professional skills.

Sabbatical leaves provide opportunities for development of research, pedagogy, artistic and professional work. Examples include focused pursuit of research grants, scholarly writing, field and laboratory research, teaching and research abroad, development of pedagogical skills, creative endeavors, and other activities relevant to university employment and professional development.

UNIVERSITY OBLIGATIONS WHILE ON SABBATICAL LEAVE

Individuals on sabbatical leave agree to resign during the term of the sabbatical from all campus obligations, including committees at unit and university levels. However, they are to maintain contact with graduate advisees or to make other arrangements so that a student's progress will not be slowed because of a faculty member's absence. Individuals on sabbatical leave are also allowed to participate in their unit's merit review system if the unit bylaws so provide.

Policy and Procedure

ASU ARIZONA STATE
UNIVERSITY WEST

Manual	Section		Number ACDW 705
Academic Affairs	Leaves and Absences		Page 2 of 6
Subject		Effective	Revised
Sabbatical Leave		2/28/1961	8/17/1997

DURATION

The sabbatical leave shall be either for one or two semesters, for academic-year applicants, or for six or twelve months, for fiscal-year applicants. If the sabbatical leave is for a full academic or fiscal year, the amount of the compensation will be three-fifths of the applicant's salary. If the sabbatical leave is for one semester or six months, compensation will be the applicant's full salary for that period. The salary awarded during a sabbatical leave is based on the contracted salary base, either for the fiscal or academic year, for the contract year during which a sabbatical leave is taken.

The fiscal or academic year during which a sabbatical leave is taken is considered the "sabbatical year," whether the leave is taken for either of the six-month periods of a fiscal-year contract, for either semester of an academic year, or for an entire fiscal or academic year.

A faculty member taking a six-month leave will arrange to be on duty for one of the two regular semesters, if a teaching assignment is involved.

CHANGES TO APPROVED SABBATICAL PROJECTS

If circumstances require that a substantial change be made in the sabbatical project after it has been approved or after the leave has begun, the applicant must obtain approval for the change from his or her dean or appropriate administrator. Failure to receive approval before making the change may result in a requirement that the individual refund part or all of the salary received during the sabbatical leave.

SUPPLEMENTAL PAY

An individual on sabbatical leave may supplement his or her compensation through fellowships, scholarships, employment, or grants-in-aid to cover expenses such as travel, secretarial assistance, tuition, research, and publication. However, the individual's total income—minus the expenses above—shall not exceed the scheduled ASU West salary for the period of the leave.

Additional compensation is to be fully explained on the sabbatical proposal form and approved before the leave is granted. Should opportunities for supplemental compensation develop after the sabbatical leave has begun or after the application form has been submitted and approved, such opportunities must be approved at the earliest opportunity through the same channels as the original proposal, excluding the unit committee.

A person on sabbatical leave may not at the same time receive supplemental funds from ASU West or through ASU West projects.

Policy and Procedure

ASU ARIZONA STATE UNIVERSITY WEST			Number ACDW 705	
Manual Academic Affairs	Section Leaves and Absences		Page .3 of 6	
Subject Sabbatical Leave		Effective 2/28/1961	Revised 8/17/1997	

RETURN TO SERVICE

An individual granted sabbatical leave is required to return to the university for a period of service equal to the length of the sabbatical leave. If he or she chooses not to return, the case will be reviewed by the proper authorities and the individual may be required to refund the amount of salary received during the period of sabbatical leave. On rare occasions when special circumstances exist, the president may recommend for Board of Regents approval that an individual have a sabbatical leave privilege even though he or she cannot return to the university for further full-time service.

An individual on sabbatical leave who accepts a tenured or tenure-track position at another postsecondary institution while on leave from ASU West will be considered to have abandoned his or her ASU West contract. In such cases, ASU West has the option of whether or not to offer a subsequent contract.

REPORT

No later than the end of the first semester after completing the sabbatical leave, the individual must submit a concise final report to the dean or appropriate administrator, addressing accomplishment of the purposes stated in the application for sabbatical leave.

Forms for the final report are available from the office of the dean or appropriate administrator. The dean/administrator will acknowledge the receipt of sabbatical reports and send copies to the vice president and provost, ASU West.

FURTHER SERVICE AND SUBSEQUENT SABBATICAL LEAVES

Following the completion of a sabbatical leave, six years of further service shall be required before an individual will become eligible to apply for a second sabbatical leave. Leaves of absence without pay for periods ordinarily not exceeding one year can be counted as periods of service towards the sabbatical leave, if the leave is for purposes related to scholarship as agreed to at the time that the leave is approved.

Time spent in the rank of full-time assistant professor or above, when the appointment is supported by local funds, shall be counted fully toward sabbatical leave if such an appointment carries the same responsibilities of teaching, research, and service normally expected of faculty members whose appointments are supported by state funds. In these cases, however, it will be necessary for the faculty member to be paid from state funds at the time the application for sabbatical leave is filed. In those cases where such appointments require that the faculty member dedicate the major share of time to sponsored research or to service required by the granting agency, the faculty member must have been paid from state funds during the three years preceding the sabbatical leave year; the faculty member must also be paid from state funds during the sabbatical year.

Policy and Procedure

ASU ARIZONA STATE UNIVERSITY WEST

Manual	Section	Number
		ACDW 705
Academic Affairs	Leaves and Absences	Page
		4 of 6

Subject	Effective	Revised
Sabbatical Leave	2/28/1961	8/17/1997

APPROVAL OF SABBATICAL LEAVES

APPLICATION SUBMISSIONS

The applicant will submit to the dean or appropriate administrator a sabbatical application form, a curriculum vitae, and any supporting data the unit requires. In addition, the appropriate administrator will obtain confidential written evaluations of the project by persons of recognized competence in the applicant's field of study. The application will be evaluated according to the following criteria:

1. probable enhancement of the applicant's effectiveness as a teacher/scholar,

2. potential value to the reputation of the unit and benefit to the institution,

3. potential contribution to knowledge and/or the dissemination of knowledge,

4. opportunity for outstanding public or professional service at a local or national, or international level, and

5. the project warrants the time requested and can be completed in that period of time.

EVALUATION OF THE APPLICATION

The dean or appropriate administrator with counsel of the appropriate unit committee will review the materials and recommend the leave if:

1. the application is judged worthwhile, based on the stated criteria,

2. there is a high probability that the applicant will succeed in doing what has been proposed and

3. the unit's program of teaching and advisement or other primary services will be maintained during the applicant's absence.

The dean or appropriate administrator will provide a positive or negative recommendation for each application. If the recommendation of the dean or appropriate administrator is negative, the applicant must be informed of the reasons for the recommendation and afforded an opportunity to respond. If the applicant responds, the vice president and provost, ASU West will consider both the recommendation of the dean or appropriate administrator and the applicant's response.

Accompanying the applications being forwarded to the vice president and provost, ASU west, the dean or appropriate administrator will submit a letter indicating how the proposed sabbatical leaves will affect the integrity of the teaching, advisement, graduate student supervision, research supervision, research, and administration of the programs within the unit.

Policy and Procedure

ASU ARIZONA STATE UNIVERSITY WEST		Number
		ACDW 705
Manual	Section	Page
Academic Affairs	Leaves and Absences	5 of 6
Subject	Effective	Revised
Sabbatical Leave	2/28/1961	8/17/1997

Following consideration of the materials and recommendations provided, the vice president and provost will approve or deny the application and will inform the dean or appropriate administrator and the applicant of the final decision and, if the decision is negative, the reasons for it.

During the final probationary year, approval of a forthcoming sabbatical leave will be contingent upon the applicant receiving tenure or continuing status.

APPLICATION DEADLINES

Applications for the following year ordinarily must be filed with the dean or appropriate administrator no later than October 5, so that applicants can be notified no later than December 7 by the vice president and provost, ASU West. If an applicant for a sabbatical leave withdraws the application or changes the period of leave after approval, the dean or appropriate administrator must be notified immediately and in sufficient time to make necessary adjustments in the teaching or service programs of the department. Applications may be withdrawn without affecting subsequent applications.

PROCEDURES

APPLICATION FOR SABBATICAL LEAVE:

RESPONSIBILITY	ACTION
Applicant	1. Submit the application form, curriculum vitae, and required supporting data to the dean or appropriate administrator.
Dean or appropriate administrator	2. Review the material and, with counsel of the appropriate committee, make a recommendation to approve or deny the request.
	If the decision is to approve the request:
	3. Skip to step 6.
	If the decision is to deny the request:
Dean or appropriate administrator	4. Inform the applicant of reasons for the recommendation.

Policy and Procedure

ASU ARIZONA STATE UNIVERSITY WEST		Number ACDW 705	
Manual Academic Affairs	Section Leaves and Absences	Page 6 of 6	
Subject Sabbatical Leave		Effective 2/28/1961	Revised 8/17/1997

APPLICATION FOR SABBATICAL LEAVE (cont.)

RESPONSIBILITY	ACTION
Applicant	5. Respond, if desired.
Dean or appropriate administrator	6. Forward all materials to vice president and provost, ASU West for consideration.
Vice president and provost, ASU West	7. Review material and make the decision to approve or deny the request.
Vice president and provost, ASU West	8. Communicate the decision to the dean or appropriate administrator and applicant.

DREW UNIVERSITY LIBRARY

SABBATICALS FOR LIBRARIANS: PROCEDURES AND POLICIES

The University Faculty Personnel Policy (UFPP) of 1979 contains the basic policy regarding sabbaticals. Specific applications for librarians follow.

The University Faculty Personnel Policy specifies: "Sabbatical leave shall be for one year at half salary or for one semester at full salary." For library faculty the equivalent periods are 5½ months at full salary or 11 months at half salary. Normally sabbatical leaves correspond to the semester schedule. Personal needs, sabbatical objective, and/or library needs may require an alternative model for a given request.

Vacation accrues in its regular manner. Vacation may or may not be part of the sabbatical leave, but the initial request should indicate the preference.

At present it appears that the library cannot sustain more than three sabbatical leaves in one year or more than 1.5 librarians on leave during any one semester. If more requests come to the Library Committee on Faculty, the committee will follow the guidelines in Review of Sabbatical Requests by the Library Committee on Faculty (November 4, 1985).

Requests should come to the Library Committee on Faculty by October 1 of the year prior to the year requested. Normally this will be an application in the sixth year of service or the sixth year since the last sabbatical, for a leave in the seventh year.

All librarians interested in applying for a sabbatical should present a brief (two page) proposal to the committee by Oct. 1 of the year preceding the proposed sabbatical year. The proposal should address the following topics.

    I.   Describe your proposed project
       A. Statement of the project
       B. Purpose or goals
       C. Methodology (where, when, what, how, etc.)
       D. Probable impact (contributions to your professional development, benefits to Drew Library or Drew University, etc.)
       E. Strategy for evaluation
       F. Funding possibilites

    II. Indicate the timing, duration, and vacation plans of your requested leave

    III. Suggest how major aspects of your job responsibilities can be met in your absence

While there is no desire to define what type of "intensive study and research" (UFPP p. 25) is appropriate for a given sabbatical, there is a sense in the committee that all projects and proposals must offer a well-reasoned argument within the range of library and/or University goals and objectives.

After returning from sabbatical one is expected to submit an evaluative report about one's sabbatical work to the committee by the next Dec. 1.

DREW UNIVERSITY LIBRARY

REVIEW OF SABBATICAL REQUESTS BY THE LIBRARY COMMITTEE ON FACULTY

The Library Committee on Faculty will review and evaluate sabbatical requests using the following procedure:

1. Determine eligibility of applicant, based on length of service and timing of previous sabbaticals. Eligibility should be in accordance with the University Faculty Personnel Policy.

2. Ensure that the proposal covers the topics outlined in the Library sabbatical procedures. This includes an adequate description of the project, the timing of the sabbatical, and arrangements for absence.

3. Determine the effect of the applicant's absence in terms of his or her responsibilities, taking into consideration any other sabbaticals proposed for the same year. The chair of LCOF should consult with the applicant's supervisor to ensure coverage of the applicant's responsibilities.

Should it appear that applicants have overlapping responsibilities, or that the proposed sabbaticals may result in more than 1.5 librarians on leave during any one semester, LCOF can suggest alternative scheduling arrangements in order to continue essential Library functions. LCOF should use the following criteria in attempting to resolve such conflicts:

> Applicant's postponement from a previous year.

> Length of service.

> Length of service since previous sabbatical.

> Ability of the Library to rearrange responsibilities of librarians on sabbatical leave.

> Outside deadlines affecting the project.

In no case should the topic of the project itself be used as a criterion.

****

Upon approval of the sabbatical requests by the Board of Trustees, the chair of LCOF should send a memo to Library staff members announcing the topics and the scheduling of forthcoming sabbaticals.

Approved by the Library Faculty, November 4, 1985.

SABBATICAL LEAVES FOR MEMBERS OF THE LIBRARY FACULTY

Revised February 1992

Members of the Library Faculty i.e. professional librarians holding full-time tenure-track appointments, are eligible to request, and to receive, sabbatical leaves as provided in Paragraphs 310.00 through 310.05 of the Gonzaga University Faculty Handbook which are incorporated by reference in faculty employment contracts. Inasmuch as library faculty members are employed on a twelve (12) month basis, and in recognition of the special operating requirements of the Library, sabbatical leaves for members of the Library Faculty will be governed by the following policies and procedures.

1.   After six (6) years of continuous service as a full-time member of the Library Faculty, a librarian holding the academic rank of Assistant Professor or higher may, and it is encouraged to, request a sabbatical leave for the purpose of study, research, writing, or other activities designed to enhance and/or improve professional effectiveness.

2.   The grant of sabbatical leave will not be automatic, but will be made at the discretion of the University administration. It is intended primarily as a means of enhancing the value of the recipient's service to the University, and each petition will be judged individually on the basis of the petitioner's achievement and promise as an academic librarian. Furthermore, the University may at times have to deny or postpone the grant of sabbatical leave because of a shortage of funds or the needs of the Library.

3.   Sabbatical leaves will normally be granted for a period of one year (12 months) or for a period of one-half year (6 months). At the request of the faculty member, and with the approval of the University administration, sabbatical leave for a period of less than six months may be authorized.

    a.   A faculty member granted a sabbatical leave of one year will be compensated at a rate of one-half his/her normal salary for that year.

    b.   A faculty member granted a sabbatical leave of one-half year or less will be compensated at a rate of his/her full salary for that period.

    c.   The Personal Leave Allowance of a faculty member granted a sabbatical leave of one-half year or less will be prorated according to the number of months worked during the remainder of the contract year in which the leave is taken.

Sabbatical Leave

4.   Sabbatical leaves are granted by the Academic Vice President upon the recommendation of the Dean of Library Services. Applications for sabbatical leave must be submitted to the Dean no later than November 1 of the year preceding the year for which leave is requested.

5.   Petitions for sabbatical leave should include the following:

        a.   The specific beginning and ending date of the proposed sabbatical leave.

        b.   A brief statement describing with reasonable specificity the proposed plan for study, research, or other activities to be pursued during the leave and how these are intended to enhance the faculty member's service to the Library and/or the University.

6.   Petitions for sabbatical leave should be accompanied by a separate statement prepared by the faculty member, in consultation with the Department Chair when applicable, which briefly assesses the anticipated impact of the faculty member's absence during the requested period of absence upon library functions/services within the faculty member's area of assigned responsibility.

7.   At the conclusion of the sabbatical leave, the faculty member shall submit a brief written report to the Dean indicating what activities were actually pursued during the period of leave and assessing the degree to which the purposes set forth in the proposal were achieved.

8.   The recipient of a sabbatical leave shall agree to remain in the service of the University for at least one year after the conclusion of the leave.

Sabbatical Leave Program

The sabbatical program is intended to provide tenured faculty members the opportunity to grow as inspiring and effective teachers and scholars. After six years of full-time service, faculty are eligible for a regular sabbatical leave for as much as one academic year, and similarly each seventh year thereafter.

The leave options are typically one semester at full benefits and salary, or a complete academic year with benefits and half salary.* Faculty members planning a sabbatical leave should consult with their department head/supervisor well in advance of the time they must file a notification of intent to apply. Both the intent-to-apply and final leave application forms are available at the end of this section. The intent-to-apply notification should be sent by the faculty proposing the leave to his/her immediate supervisor by April 1 (or the first weekday thereafter), approximately 16 months before the beginning of the academic year in which the leave is requested. By this time the faculty member should be discussing tentative plans for use of the sabbatical semester/year so that a well-developed plan can be completed by the fall deadline for final application. The supervisor should sign the notification form and forward one copy to the Provost and one copy to the Associate Dean of the Faculty by May 1 (or the first weekday thereafter).

<u>Application Guidelines and Requirements</u>

1. A copy of the final leave application should be submitted by the faculty member to his/her immediate supervisor by October 15, approximately 10 months prior to the beginning of the academic year during which the leave is requested. Final applications, along with supporting letters are due in the Associate Dean's office on November 1.

2. The narrative portion should begin with a one-paragraph abstract suitable for publication and dissemination to faculty colleagues and to the IWU Board of Trustees. The body of the narrative is normally 3-5 pages.

   Important note to applicants: The narrative should be skillfully written. Considering the likely lack of expertise of most FDC members in the applicant's field of endeavor, applicants should emphasize the idea or question to be studied, the methodology to be used, and the significance of the work to the scholarly/artistic community. Proposals should be comprehensible to the non-specialist so as to allow FDC members to assess the quality, significance, and feasibility of the project. Technical or highly discipline-specific content and references, if any, should be included in an appendix.

3. The narrative should:

   - specify the objectives of the proposed leave
   - explain in some detail how these objectives/goals will be reached as a result of the leave
   - indicate the importance of the proposed leave to the applicant's personal and professional development as a teacher and a scholar
   - summarize the applicant's record of accomplishment on previously IWU-funded grants and leaves

4. The applicant's immediate supervisor should send a letter of evaluation and recommendation to the Associate Dean of the Faculty by November 1 (or the first weekday thereafter). The supervisor's letter is an important source of information and a valuable aid in evaluating leave proposals. **The supervisor should provide a critical review of the leave proposal, understandable to the non-specialist, rather than a general endorsement.** FDC asks that the supervisor include the following in his/her evaluation:

   - the significance of the leave's objectives in the discipline or field
   - the importance of the leave for the applicant's professional development as a teacher and/or scholar
   - an assessment of the applicant's record of accomplishment on previous grants and leaves
   - the staffing plan for replacing the applicant's teaching responsibilities.

5. All research involving the use of animals or human subjects must receive approval from the proper institutional review committee. FDC must receive notification of approval before a sabbatical will be granted, although leaves may be recommended to the Provost provisionally, pending the completion of the approval process.

   See the IWU *Faculty Handbook* (available at http://www.iwu.edu/melloncenter) for details on policies governing the use of animals or human subjects. Approval forms for submitting projects involving animals may be obtained from Professor James Dougan, Psychology Department, x3415; forms for submitting projects using human subjects can be obtained from the Office of the Associate Provost, x3255.

6. All applicants should submit a current curriculum vitae. In addition, applicants who have received Artistic and Scholarly Development funding should provide information on the outcomes (publications, presentations, performances, etc.) of that funding.

7. The faculty member should submit 6 copies of the complete application to the Associate Dean of the Faculty by the November deadline. If the nature of the sabbatical leave project could be significantly altered after this deadline (e.g., if external funding is required for all or part of the leave and the status of the funding is uncertain) the applicant should indicate how his/her leave schedule could be affected.

Review Procedures and Reporting Requirements

The Associate Dean of the Faculty will forward all elements of the proposal and the supervisor's evaluation to FDC for its careful review.

The Provost will meet with the Associate Dean and members of FDC and will consult with the President before final sabbatical recommendations are made to the Board of Trustees at the February meeting. Applicants will be notified soon after that meeting, and they must make formal acceptance of a leave in writing within 30 days. It is normally expected that the faculty member will return for a full academic year of service after the sabbatical.*

A written summary of the completed leave program is due on November 1 (or the first weekday thereafter) for leaves taken the previous academic year. There is no formal report form, but a written report of scholarly and professional activities undertaken during the leave and the relation of those activities to the original proposal must be filed with the Associate Dean of the Faculty. **This report becomes an important part of FDC's evaluation of an applicant's future grant and leave proposals.**

*_Important Note:_ Financial arrangements and other details are specified in a formal leave contract between the faculty member and the university. The policy stated above reflects current (1999-2000) sabbatical compensation. FDC is working with the Provost to study the possibility of enhanced pay for full-year leaves after a faculty member's first sabbatical. It is possible, although by no means certain, that such an enhanced salary program could be available to applicants planning sabbaticals in 2000-2001._

LINFIELD COLLEGE
APPLICATION FOR SABBATICAL LEAVE

Please submit all six parts of this application as described below to the Dean's Office prior to this year's announced deadline. **Enclose also a résumé.)**

I.   Biographical Information

Name _____ Date _____

Academic Rank and Title _____

Highest academic earned degree _____Year _____

Number of years at Linfield on full-time appointment _____

Year of last Linfield sabbatical _____

Year of last leave of absence _____

Years remaining (as of end of the present academic year) before anticipated date of retirement _____

II. Requested Sabbatical Leave

        _____Year at **half** salary
        academic year: _____
        _____One semester at full salary
        fall of (year) _____
        spring of (year) _____

III. Brief Description of Proposed Sabbatical Project

A.   Descriptive title _____

B.   Concise Summary _____

_____

_____

_____

_____

_____

_____

_____

_____

_____

IV. Detailed Description of the Project

In the space below and on such additional pages as may be required, please describe in detail the project you wish to carry out during the proposed sabbatical leave. Please make the description of your project and its significance as understandable as you can for a reader who will most likely not be in your field. Indicate what outcomes you will take to indicate a successful project at the conclusion of your sabbatical.

IX–78

V. Benefit to College

Sabbatical leaves are granted at Linfield because it is believed that an appropriate sabbatical leave project benefits the College. Possible benefits include strengthening the instructional program and enhancing the reputation of the College. Describe below the benefit(s) to the College you believe will ensue from your proposed sabbatical leave.

VI. Department Chairperson's Statement

This application must include a statement by the department chairperson that (a) that the department endorses the application and finds the possible negative effects of our absence to be acceptable, and (b) presents a proposal as to how your teaching and non-committee responsibilities should be handled in your absence. Please inform your chairperson of what is required and attach his or her signed statement.

Sabbaticals

The university provides five sabbaticals annually to encourage active professional growth on the part of the faculty. These sabbaticals will normally be awarded for one semester and provide as a stipend the salary which the teacher would have been paid for teaching during the semester. (All fringe benefits will continue.) The minimum time and energy a recipient devotes to these awards must be *equal to a normal semester's work*. Applicants who expect to be engaged in other work during the semester (compensated or not) must notify the committee of the possibility and document the fact that such work will not interfere with the completion of the proposed project.

To be eligible, applicants must have served as full-time members of the faculty for a minimum of six years (excluding the year of the proposed sabbatical).

Applications for awards must be submitted by February 15 on forms which are available in the provost's office or on O:\ACAD\DEAN\Sabbatical.apl. Before review by the Sabbatical Committee, applications must be approved by the department chair and dean of the college. (Chair's Endorsement Form or its equivalency is due on or before February 15. If the applicant is a department chair, he/she is asked to submit the completed Chair's Form directly to the dean for approval.) For scheduling purposes, those intending to apply for a sabbatical must declare their intent to department chairs on or before January 15 of that year. Although it is possible to apply for a fall sabbatical, the spring semester is preferable due to the greater student demand in the fall. In any case, this should be orchestrated with the department chair.

Normally no more than one faculty member from a department will be awarded a sabbatical in a particular semester. A faculty member who has received a sabbatical is ineligible to receive it again for six years. (A recipient in 1999-2000 would not be eligible to receive an award again until 2006-07.) Unless explicitly understood and stated in writing to the contrary, an individual who requests and receives a sabbatical incurs an obligation to return to the university for at least one year immediately following such leave.

Compensated Educational/Professional Leave

A compensated educational/professional leave of up to one (1) year is available to all full-time administrative employees.

The Order of Saint Benedict recognizes that it is important for Administrative employees to keep abreast of developments and trends in their areas of responsibility and to acquire new skills and knowledge that are directly applicable to their areas of responsibility or future responsibility.

Definition

A compensated educational/professional leave is defined as an absence of one (1) to twelve (12) (not necessarily consecutive) months, for the purpose of study, training, or research in activities related to the administrative employee's work.

Eligibility

An administrative employee is eligible to apply for a long-term, compensated educational leave after seven (7) years of continuous service. The employee is eligible for subsequent leaves after an additional seven (7) year period of employment.

Salaries

Administrative employees on compensated educational leave will be paid at the following rates:

leave of 50% or less of contract or appointment will be at full salary;

leave of 51% to 75% of contract or appointment will be paid 3/4 salary;

leave of 76% to full contract or appointment will be paid at 1/2 salary.

The administrative employee will not accept any other employment that might interfere with the proposed leave plan. However, employment compatible with the leave--and any fellowships or grants--may be accepted if total compensation (the Order of Saint Benedict and other employment) does not exceed the employee's annual Order of Saint Benedict compensation. If, after reasonable project expenses have been taken into consideration, the total compensation exceeds the employee's normal salary, the leave stipend will be reduced by the excess amount.

The employee continues to participate fully in all benefit programs for which he or she is eligible; the corporation will continue its matching contributions.

The administrative position will be held for the employee upon return from leave, and the employee is expected to return to full-time employment for at least one (1) year following a long-term compensated educational leave.

Procedures

Request should be given by October 1 for the next fiscal year. Notification of acceptance or rejection will be given after the budget for the next fiscal year has been approved, which could be up to six (6) months.

The employee who wishes to request a long-term compensated educational leave obtains the pertinent application forms from the Human Resources Office, which at the time the forms are requested determines the employee's eligibility to apply. The completed application is returned to the Human Resources Office.

The application for this leave must state:

the specific purpose of the leave;

the advantage(s) to the individual and to the corporation;

together with the proposed duration of the leave.

The request must be accompanied by recommendations from the person's immediate supervisor and the administrative manager of the department involved, provided that neither is the Executive-in-Charge. These recommendations must include a statement covering the ways in which the employee's workload can be handled during the proposed absence.

The employee should file a copy of the request and materials with the Chair of the Administrative Assembly Steering Committee.

These groups will give the appropriate administrative group information concerning the types and number of leave requests and in rare cases of conflict or of repeated non-acceptance of a quality request to formally support an individual request.

Criteria for Selection

In general, acceptance of a request for leave will depend upon the following criteria:

the professional content of the proposal

a strong relationship to the employee's area of current or future responsibility

timeliness-coincidental opportunities that might be:

* external (e.g., a grant opportunity or the beginning of a program not usually available)

* internal (e.g., restructuring of a department)

* personal (e.g., spouse also on leave)

Approval Process

The Executive-in-Charge reviews the application and makes a recommendation to the President or the Chief Administrative Officer for appropriate action. After approval from the President at Saint John's University, the request is forwarded to the Board. Judgments are rendered on an individual basis by the Board of Regents or its Executive Committee.

The President or other Chief Administrative Officer considers the leave within the limits of the division's ability to sustain its normal operation during the employee's absence, as well as the financial requirements necessary to support both the leave-taker and a possible replacement.

For Joint positions, both Executives-in-Charge or the Provost and both Presidents must approve.

Sabbaticals and Leaves

A. Full-time professors, associate professors, and assistant professors who have taught at the College for at least six years are eligible for consideration for sabbatical leaves. Requests should be addressed to the Dean and transmitted with a recommendation by the chairman of the department or division concerned. Such leaves shall not occur more often than one year in every seven. The first sabbatical will normally be granted after six years of service; subsequent sabbaticals may be granted any year during the normal cycle of seven years to enable faculty to undertake special projects of a timely nature, or to accommodate the College's overall staffing needs. To the extent possible, sabbatical leaves should be arranged without the necessity of appointing sabbatical replacements.

    1. Comparable eligibility extends to administrative officers at the level of dean, vice-president, director, or librarians with faculty status provided that the purpose of the leave is related to increasing professional skills. Leaves of four months (one regular term) or less may be requested with full salary; leaves up to nine months may be requested at half-salary. Leaves without salary may also be requested.

    2. Request for faculty and administrative leave should be submitted no later than October 15 of the academic year preceding that in which the leave is sought.

B. The beneficiary of a sabbatical leave may request a full year leave with half salary or a half-year leave with full salary. The leave is contingent upon satisfactory arrangements being made for the teaching program of the department. Those receiving a sabbatical leave are expected to return to the College for a least one full year of service following the leave.

C. Since a sabbatical leave is granted for the purpose of both encouraging continued scholarship and renewing teaching effectiveness, it is expected that the major part of a sabbatical leave will be taken off campus and will be devoted to study, writing, travel, or other activity designed to accomplish this dual purpose. A faculty member wishing to teach during a sabbatical should obtain permission to do so in advance from the departmental chairman and the Dean. A statement should be prepared explaining the specific advantages foreseen. On return a brief written report of the sabbatical leave shall be presented to the Dean.

D. The granting of leave is at the discretion of the President, after consultation with the department or division concerned and with the Dean. Sabbatical leave is not granted automatically but only with due concern for the best interests of the College.

E. The President shall have the discretion to grant a special leave of absence, without remuneration, to a member of the faculty for the completion of the doctorate or for the pursuit of other scholarly activities which will contribute to the individual's professional competence. Such special leaves shall not be counted as service to the College in calculating eligibility for sabbatical leave unless the initiative has been taken by the College in arranging the special leave.

F. The granting of a sabbatical leave shall not exclude the faculty member from consideration for promotion and/or average salary increase and/or any other normal increases in faculty benefits to become effective during the period of absence.

G. The College will continue making contributions for fringe benefits, except for the contributions to the retirement program, of all faculty members on leave of absence under a grant or fellowship, but will not pay for those on personal leave without pay. (See above procedures relating to approved leave.)

Travel Reimbursement Policies

Alma College
Alma, Michigan

Southwest Baptist University
Bolivar, Missouri

Alma College
Travel Related Expense Reimbursement Policies

<u>Alma College Travel Expenses</u>: Reasonable and necessary business related expenses incurred by employees while traveling on Alma College business are paid by the College. In most cases this is done on a reimbursement basis. The fundamentals of expense account policy are simple common sense. If an employee travels on College business, he/she will be reimbursed within the College travel policies for his/her travel expenses. As with any other expenditure, the College expects to receive value for the expenditure. Travel and entertainment must be intended to accomplish specific business objectives and those objectives documented on the expense report.

<u>Air Travel</u>: As a rule, all air travel on behalf of the College shall be coach. The "lowest logical airfare" (even including stopovers or connecting flights) shall be pursued with the travel agency prior to departure. Employees are encouraged to take advantage of super saver discounts when they make sense.

<u>Hotel</u>: Employees should stay at moderately priced hotels or book through travel agencies that offer corporate rates. The College encourages the use of our negotiated discount program through the Choice Hotels International (Sleep Inn, Comfort Inn, Quality Inn, Clarion, EconoLodge, Roadway Inn and Friendship Inn). Our corporate membership number is 00947768 and will result in either a 15% or 20% discount for all reservations booked through the toll free number 1-800-258-2847. In addition, through discussions with the Marriott chain, they have identified that we are eligible for a corporate rate if requested upon making the reservation. These vary by hotel but should be somewhere in the range of 5% to 26 % off the published book rates. When making reservations at other hotels, please ask if there are corporate rates available. They may be able to give you a discount under one of their existing programs.

Employees are encouraged to select a hotel close to their destination with a sensitivity to hotel accommodations, cost, mileage, and stewardship of time.

Reasonable tips for hotel baggage handling are allowable.

<u>Car Rental</u>: Only if extensive travel is required should a car rental be necessary. Optional insurance coverage should be waived as College policies provide adequate coverage. Be sure to refuel before returning in order to avoid surcharges. College insurance information is available from the office of the Vice President for Finance and Administration.

<u>Expense Advances</u>: Historically, the College has issued travel advances as a result of not having a corporate credit card program. Effective in 1999 the College initiated a corporate credit card program through MasterCard. These cards are available to faculty and administrators who travel on a regular basis. While it is a

corporate card program, the individual faculty or staff cardholder is responsible for the entire balance for items charged on the card. Reimbursable expenses are governed by other provisions in our travel policies.

For those who do not have an Alma College corporate credit card, a travel advance up to the amount of anticipated reimbursable expenses for the trip may be requested in advance from the Business Office. Travel advance requests should be submitted to the Business Office by Wednesday noon to receive a check on Friday. A travel advance should be requested on a regular requisition form with your supervisor's approval. Such advances are accounted for in the trip expense report.

Expense Reports: These must have the approval of the employee's respective supervisor or department manager. They may be submitted at the end of the trip or at the end of each month, but no later than 30 days after the date of the expenditure.

Meals and Beverages: Employees traveling on Alma College business may request reimbursement for meals up to the following amounts:

	REGULAR	HIGH COST CITIES
Breakfast	$ 6.00	$ 8.00
Lunch	9.00	12.00
Dinner	15.00	25.00

A number of cities have been identified as high cost and, therefore, higher meal allowances have been established. These cities are Boston, Chicago, Dallas, Denver, Los Angeles, New York City, San Francisco, Seattle, and Washington, D.C.

These amounts are inclusive of tips. If an employee is traveling for an entire day, where the employee is entitled to reimbursement for all three meals, it is acceptable to use the total daily amount in a different combination than noted above. For example, it would be permissible to spend $5.00 each on breakfast and lunch, and $20.00 on dinner. These amounts are for reimbursable meal expenses only and are not simply allowances for being away to be used on other personal expenditures. Meals already paid for by the College as part of conference fees are not reimbursable. Complimentary continental breakfasts should be taken advantage of if possible, and are not reimbursable.

Parking, Toll Roads And Bridges: Expenses for these items are reimbursable subject to the receipt requirements below.

Entertainment: If an employee entertains others for a good business reason, he/she will be reimbursed for those expenses. The reimbursement in these cases is not subject to the meal and beverage maximums. The expense reimbursement report must include the person(s) entertained, the location, and the business purpose. As with any other expenditure, the College expects to receive value for the expenditure. If there are any questions on the use of College funds for entertaining expenses, the employee is encouraged to consult the sector vice president ahead of time.

Receipt Requirements: Receipts must be provided for all meal expenses, lodging expenses or any other expenditure over $5. Lodging expenses must be supported by a detailed billing statement. Airline ticket stubs are required for reimbursement of airline charges. Credit card receipts or printed cash register tapes are required for meals and other expenses. When prior arrangements are made with the Business Office, certain hand logs or per-diem allowances may be allowed. These arrangements are made primarily for group travel programs.

Auto Expenses: Employees are encouraged to use College vehicles when available. Employees may be authorized to use personal cars for occasional travel on College business. They will be reimbursed at the current rate, which may change annually. Mileage between home and the office is considered personal mileage and is not reimbursable. Employees with a College vehicle assigned to them are not eligible for reimbursement of mileage on their personal car. The College does not provide any insurance on personal vehicles, even when used for College business.

Other: Expenses for hotels, meals, etc. beyond the business purpose of the trip are personal expenses and, therefore, are not reimbursable. The exception to this would be in the case of an airfare super saver where the airfare savings are greater than the additional costs of extending the stay.

One personal call is allowed at College expense if the employee is gone from home on College business for five or more consecutive days. In lieu of a dollar limit on this call, employees are encouraged to use reasonable judgement (5-10 minutes).

Some employees own personal cell phones and occasionally choose to use those for College business calls. It is appropriate for the employee to be reimbursed for the charges related to that individual business call. These reimbursements may include airtime, long distance charges and/or roaming charges.

These policies are for employee expenses only. Additional expenses incurred for a spouse or guest are the responsibility of the individual.

2.6 **TRAVEL REIMBURSEMENT POLICY**

The policy of Southwest Baptist University is to reimburse employees and others for expenses incurred while on official university business.

The following regulations will guide the approval of and reimbursement for travel expense incurred by employees or persons traveling for the interest of the University in the performance of official duties:

2.6.1 Availability of Funds

It will be the responsibility of the supervisor to ascertain that sufficient funds are available before authorizing reimbursable travel expenses.

2.6.2 Approval for Travel

No individual will be reimbursed for travel expense unless he/she has obtained prior approval from the supervisor to incur such expense and has submitted the proper travel vouchers in good order.

A. Authorization may be given for recurring expense within a specified time period not to exceed the fiscal year.

B. If funding for the expense is not under the authority of the appropriate supervisor, prior written authorization is also required from the person responsible for the account to which the expenses are to be charged.

2.6.3 Definition of Reimbursable Expenses

In general, only the actual expenses deemed necessary and reasonable by the supervisor will be reimbursed. There will be, however, no deviation from the specific regulations outlined below.

2.6.4 Reimbursable Expenditures Items

A. Transportation--Travel expenses include those incurred by moving from place to place by automobile, air, bus, or train.

1. Automobile travel is incurred when using a personal vehicle, hired vehicle or taxi. These charges will be reimbursed but require documentation reporting dates and destinations of each trip.

2. Air travel must be approved in advance by the supervisor with a full description of destination and purpose of the trip. Air travel to destinations within 400 miles from Bolivar, Missouri, shall be reimbursed at 20 cents per ground mile, in a round trip from Bolivar to the destination. Air travel beyond 400 miles shall be reimbursed for actual expenses incurred for coach class.

3. Bus travel and rail travel shall be reimbursed for actual expenses incurred with a description of the destination and purpose of each trip.

4. When using a personal vehicle, travel will be reimbursed at the rate of 20 cents per mile regardless of the number of passengers.

5. Parking, garage and toll charges will be reimbursed if considered necessary, but must substantiated with documentation.
6. No other charges will be allowed, i.e., repairs, oil, gas, etc.
7. Mileage traveled will be reported on the travel voucher in the space provided and utilized to determine the total of the expenditure.

The University will reimburse any employee for any expense related to renting an automobile when such expense is reasonable and more economical than taxi and other modes of transportation; however, it is necessary when renting a vehicle that the policies on travel insurance listed in 2.6.7 be followed.

B.   Meals

As a general rule, receipts must be presented on travel vouchers for all meals. However, the following per diem schedule does not require receipts:

    Daily rate $25
    Partial rates
        Breakfast . . . . $ 5
        Lunch . . . . $ 6
        Dinner $14

Partial rates should be used when every meal is not to be reimbursed, e.g., travel begins after lunch, conference fees include dinner and breakfast, or travel ends before dinner. Expenses in excess of the per diem rate are deemed to be the exception and are to be verified by a receipt.

C.   Lodging

University employees are expected to seek "reasonable" lodging. An itemized statement furnished by the hotel is required for reimbursement of actual costs. Employees are encouraged to made advance registration and seek to secure potential discounts.

D.   Miscellaneous

The University will reimburse, from receipts, for all miscellaneous expenses related to the pursuit of business purposes while away from campus, which shall include the following:

1. laundry services for shirts, blouses and personal items (when away from campus for more than three consecutive nights) and
2. one personal phone call of reasonable length per day and telephone facsimile services related to university business.

2.6.5   Non-reimbursable Expenditures

Non-reimbursable expenditures include the following:

A.   a meal in Bolivar involving only SBU employees;
B.   candy, gum, breath mints, etc.;
C.   entertainment (movie in hotel/motel room, theme parks, etc.), except as provided in the University procedures manual for students on extended trips;

D.   as a general rule, expenditures for a spouse or other dependents while accompanying the employee on university business; and

E.   gifts for employees.

2.6.6   <u>Expense Report</u>

Expense reports may be filed monthly or immediately after travel. The following should be specifically included:

A.   The date and purpose of the travel and destination should be clearly identified.

B.   Meetings or organizations should be identified by full name rather than by the common acronym.

C.   Lodging expenses may be summarized for the travel period. However, an itemized statement from the hotel must be attached.

D.   Expenses other than transportation, lodging, and meals are to be itemized. The type and amount of expense is to be listed separately and must include receipts.

E.   Unusual expenses are to be documented.

F.   Individuals other than the one submitting the report for whom expenses are incurred are to be identified.

G.   Expenses incurred locally are reimbursable only when it is for the benefit of the University.

H.   Expenses for family members are generally not reimbursable and are to be reimbursed only when such expenses are for the benefit of the University. These expenditures must be approved (in advance) by the supervisor. Expenses in this and other areas relating to the President will be approved and reviewed in accordance with policies established by the Chairman of the Board of Trustees.

I.   In order to receive reimbursement, the person submitting the claim must sign the travel voucher.

OT 73 X 219

110 - Travel Reimbursement Policies